GOING
UNDERGROUND

GOING UNDERGROUND

Your Guide to Caves in the Mid-Atlantic

Sharon Hernes Silverman

CAMINO BOOKS, INC.
Philadelphia

Manufactured in the United States of America

1 2 3 4 5 94 93 92 91

Library of Congress Cataloging-in-Publication Data

Silverman, Sharon Hernes.
    Going Underground: your guide to caves in the Mid-Atlantic
by Sharon Hernes Silverman.
      p. cm.
      1. Caves—Middle Atlantic States—Guide books. 2. Middle Atlantic
States—Description and travel—Guide books.
      I. Title.
      GB605.M55S55 1991

551.4'47'02575—dc20   91-12886

ISBN 0-940159-12-0

**This book is available at a special discount on bulk purchases for promotional,
business and educational use.
For information, write to:**

Publisher
Camino Books, Inc.
P.O. Box 59026
Philadelphia, PA 19102

CONTENTS

I am grateful to the National Caves Association and the National Speleological Society for the valuable information they provided. My thanks also, to the cave owners, operators and tour guides in New York, Pennsylvania, Maryland, Virginia, and West Virginia who completed questionnaires, responded to requests for historical and geologic data, supplied background information and showed me through their beautiful caves.

I would like to express my appreciation to Dr. Calvin L. Moyer for the permanent loan of his library on caves and caving; to Edward Jutkowitz of Camino Books; to the Philadelphia Writers' Organization; to my parents, Babe and Seymour Hernes; to the entire Hernes and Silverman families, especially Helene H. Silverman and Barry Silverman; and to my friends and advisors, notably Peter Bakalian and Judith Ritcher.

My husband, Alan B. Silverman, accompanied me on many cave ours and took most of the photographs that appear in this book. He deserves thanks not only for that, but for the love and enthusiasm that made this project a reality and makes our life together a joy.

And to all of you who are about to venture underground, my thanks in advance for treating the beautiful-and fragile-cave environment with care and respect.

INTRODUCTION

A spectacular shield formation at Grand Caverns, Virginia.

Welcome to the wonderful world of caves! You are about to enter an underground environment whose beauty rivals anything found on the surface. Gleaming speleothems (formations), crystal-clear pools, and gigantic subterranean rooms offer the opportunity for adventure and exploration; developed caves have good pathways and lighting to make this thrill a safe one.

WHAT'S IN THIS BOOK

A tourist can visit all the caves in this book without any special equipment. Every cave in New York, Pennsylvania, Maryland, West Virginia, and Virginia is listed here. (There are no tourist caves in New Jersey or Delaware.)

For each cave, the following information is included: cave name, location, mailing address, telephone number, admission fee and available discounts, whether credit cards and personal checks are accepted, season and hours, maximum number of people per tour, duration of tour, whether the cave is wheelchair accessible, special events, on-site facilities, driving directions, and local attractions. These facts should help you make travel plans, whether you intend to visit one cave or many.

In addition, a brief history of the cave is provided along with a description of some of the more notable features and an assessment of the tour. Descriptions of how caves, even those not found in the mid-Atlantic area, form and of speleothems are included along with a glossary of terms to help you become an informed cave visitor, thereby increasing your appreciation of just how incredible caves are.

Not content to depend solely on information furnished by cave owners and operators, I personally visited every cave in this book; my husband and I took the photographs. To verify that the facts were accurate at press time, I sent a detailed questionnaire to each cave manager prior to the 1991 season. Although I have endeavored to make this guidebook complete and error-free, it is inevitable that some information (notably hours and admission fees) will change; for that reason I encourage you to contact caves directly by phone or by mail when planning your visit.

HOW TO DRESS

Cave temperature approximates the average annual temperature of the ground above. Temperatures for the caves listed in this book are in the 45° to 55°F range, so bring a sweater or sweatshirt.

Although developed caves offer safe walkways, often paved, sometimes the caves can be muddy. Wear sneakers or other suitable walking shoes, and don't wear a good pair of pants unless you don't mind getting them dirty.

FOR MORE INFORMATION

For additional information about the caves listed in this book (and other show caves in the United States), contact:

National Caves Association
Route 9, Box 106
McMinnville, TN 37110

For information about spelunking (cave exploration), contact:

National Speleological Society
Cave Avenue
Huntsville, AL 35810

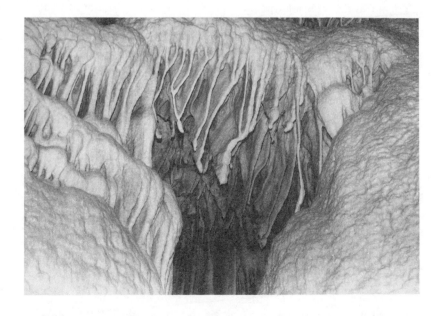

Sparkling speleothems at Indian Echo Caverns, Pennsylvania.

Many types of formations decorate Shenandoah Caverns, Virginia.

Chemical and mechanical processes create underground splendor.

HOW CAVES FORM

LIMESTONE CAVES

The genesis of limestone caves is a testimony to the awesome power of water, and to nature's perpetual quest for equilibrium. Chemically (through dissolution) and mechanically (through abrasion and erosion), water is responsible for carving limestone caves. It is water, too, that produces the glistening speleothems, also called "formations," that decorate the caves later in their life cycle.

The process begins, appropriately enough, with limestone. An accumulation of organic remains such as shells, coral, and marine life under ancient oceans furnishes calcium carbonate, or calcite, the main ingredient of limestone. Geological changes over millions of years then force this sedimentary rock up as the seas drain away, leaving vast areas of limestone just under the earth's surface. A large limestone region exists in the middle Atlantic states.

Limestone can be dissolved by mildly acid water, so the next step in cave formation is for rainwater to become acidic. It does this by slowly percolating through the soil (the water is called "groundwater" at this point), picking up carbon dioxide, a product of plant decay and animal respiration, along the way. When carbon dioxide combines with groundwater, it forms a weak acid called "carbonic acid," H_2CO_3. It is this acid that dissolves limestone.

The water table lies close to the surface now, and there may be an underground river. As the slightly acid water seeps through cracks, it dissolves small cavities in the saturated area below the water table, the geological equivalent of tooth decay. As the river sinks to a deeper level, the cavities enlarge and join together. Floods periodically scour and enlarge the cracks and openings.

Over thousands of years, the river sinks deeper underground. The old cave above is no longer filled with water, and a new system of caves forms along the new, lower water table. Draining water connects the upper and lower cave systems by boring vertical shafts through the limestone. As you tour caves, you may notice these multiple levels, walking on the uppermost dry one while observing the wetter, perhaps flooded cave system below.

As the caves erode and enlarge, the seeping groundwater continues its journey through the soil, absorbing carbon dioxide gas along the way. Because the amount of calcium carbonate that can be dissolved increases with the amount of carbon dioxide in the water, the water dissolves the limestone until it is saturated with calcium carbonate.

Finally the drop of water ends up hanging from the roof of an open cave passage, surrounded by the atmosphere of the cave.

Cave air is chemically very like normal outside air: both have a low carbon dioxide content, much lower than that of "soil" air. But the drop of water has accumulated a large proportion of carbon dioxide during its passage through the soil. Therefore, it is out of equilibrium, and carbon dioxide must diffuse from the water into the cave air to restore stability.

As it does so, the calcium carbonate content of the water is thrown out of balance, so it precipitates out of the water as calcite to maintain the gas-mineral equilibrium. This is the initial stage in the formation of a stalactite. Before equilibrium is reached, the drop is pushed off the roof by water above it, falls to the floor and deposits what's left of its still excessive load of calcite. This calcite deposit is the beginning of a stalagmite.

Next, the water runs downhill over the cave floor toward an underground stream. The cascading water now wears away the limestone mechanically. The powerfully surging water scours and chips at the walls while still carrying dissolved limestone. Often a canyon is cut through the rock. The water eventually slows down as it reaches the saturated zone of the new water table. The pressure of water behind it keeps it moving forward toward an exit. Eventually the stream flows out of the cave at a spring, carrying its dissolved load of limestone toward the sea.

Limestone caves are generally less than ten million years old, even when the rock that surrounds them formed hundreds of millions of years ago.

ICE CAVES

Ice caves are natural deep-freeze areas for the cold air of winter. They allow ice to persist through most of the summer and fall.

The existence of these strange caves can actually be explained quite simply. Ice caves are usually located in areas with severe winters and short summers. Even in warm weather, the rock covering the cave acts as insulation against the sun and summer air.

In winter, heavy cold air settles to the cave's lowest level, where it cannot be displaced by lighter, warmer air. With constant below-freezing temperatures, moisture in the air condenses into blankets of frost on rock surfaces. Icicles and frost crystals glisten on the walls of ice caves; dripping water creates ice stalagmites and slippery floors. Occasionally, underground glaciers form.

Since a cave's temperature approximates the average annual temperature above ground, ice is fairly common in caves at high elevations in northern areas, especially in shallow lava tubes that trap cold air. Even at lower elevations, like Ice Caves Mountain in New York, ice may remain all year because a cave is aligned in such a way that it, too, acts as a cold trap. Each winter and spring more cold air and water replenish the ice in the cave.

GYPSUM CAVES

Softer and more soluble than limestone, gypsum is composed of hydrated calcium sulphate. Occasionally, large caverns form in gypsum in much the same way as caves form in limestone, although they rarely attain the awesome dimensions of limestone caves.

Gypsum can form flower-like speleothems in limestone caves; in addition, it sometimes appears on the floor of limestone caves in the form of needles and crystals.

Commercially, gypsum is used for plaster of paris and plasterboard. Another economically useful form of gypsum—alabaster—is also found in caves.

LAVA CAVES

Lava caves or tubes present a classic example of the extrusion process. Forming quickly (geologically speaking), lava caves result when a flowing stream of lava cools and solidifies on the outside. Since the core is still hot and liquid, an underlying tongue of molten lava continues to flow below the surface. When the liquid lava drains from the interior and the walls cool and harden completely, a tubular cavity remains.

Lava caves usually do not come with ready-made openings. An entrance to a lava cave typically forms when part of the ceiling collapses after the lava cools.

The tubes can be up to several miles long, branching upstream and downstream of the direction of lava flow. Later flow may refill the tubes.

SANDSTONE CAVES

Sandstone, a sedimentary rock (usually quartz) held together with silica, iron oxide, or calcium carbonate, is easily eroded by the elements. Look at any photograph of the imposing sandstone cliffs of the southwestern United States and you'll notice that the rockface is pitted with shallow holes. It is this same action by weather that causes true caves to form in sandstone.

Sandstone caves form at the bases of cliffs, where the rock may be less well cemented together than higher up. Flowing water and wind erode the stone and dissolve the cement, causing the sand grains to fall apart. Rivers can carve deep hollows that leave large overhangs above. Interestingly, the sandstone higher up may actually become tougher because additional material is deposited on its surface via capillary action.

While limestone caves are too wet, cold, and dark to provide comfortable accommodations, sandstone caves were often inhabited by early man. They offered shelter from the elements and protection from enemies.

SEA CAVES

Sea caves form in a similar fashion to sandstone caves: they are carved by the constant pounding of surf against weak spots in the rocks.

The primary difference is that sandstone is easily eroded, while rocks along the coast are often very hard. Nevertheless, these cliffs are no match for the powerful abrasive actions of water, sand, and wind as they continually pummel and grind.

Most sea caves are shallow, with daylight penetrating to the deepest reaches of the caves. They are sometimes notable for the visiting animal life, including sea lions.

Stalactite meets stalagmite at Endless Caverns, Virginia.

SPELEOTHEMS, OR CAVE DECORATIONS

Cave decorations formed when secondary minerals are deposited are often called "formations." However, geologists use the word "formation" to mean "how caves form." A specific term that applies only to cave decorations is "speleothem," from the Greek *spelaion* (cave) and *thema* (deposit). The word applies only to deposits formed form a chemical solution or by the solidification of a fluid after a cave has been formed. Sand and mud are deposited in large quantities, but they rarely develop interesting shapes (except for an occasional mud stalagmite).

Dozens of different minerals are found in limestone caves, but it is calcite that forms the greatest variety of beautiful cave decorations.

Stalactites and soda straws at Massanutten Caverns, Virginia.

Slightly acid water percolates downward from the soil zone and enters the cave. This water deposits the calcite it holds in solution, contributing to the formation of a speleothem. Among the sulphate minerals, gypsum (hydrated calcium sulphate) is the most common.

Cave deposits fall into two general categories: dripstone and flowstone. Dripstone speleothems form when water drips from a crack in the cave's ceiling. Flowstone speleothems are caused by the flowing movement of water over a cave's ceiling, walls, or floor.

STALACTITES AND SODA STRAWS

Stalactites are the icicle-like dripstone speleothems that hang from cave ceilings. Each stalactite begins as a single drop of water that forms on the ceiling after becoming saturated with calcite from the limestone above. When the water reaches the air in the cave chamber, carbon dioxide diffuses out and a ring of calcite is deposited.

As additional drops follow the same path, hanging onto the calcite left by the previous one, more rings form until a slender tube hangs from the ceiling. These tubes are known as "soda straws," because their diameter and wall thickness are about the same as a drinking straw. Straws occasionally grow up to 10 feet long before breaking off.

The uniform shape of soda straws occurs because water flows down the inside of the tube and does not meet the cave air until it reaches the tip. Every time a new layer is added to the end of the tube, the molecules are precisely laid down in the same crystalline pattern as the previous layer. The tube has the same structure as a single calcite crystal would.

Often the tiny hole is not large enough to carry all the water coming from above, or becomes clogged. This causes the water to flow down the outside of the tube, depositing a layer of calcite and forming a stalactite.

Stalactites come in many shapes, depending on mineral content, water flow rate, and the diffusion rate of carbon dioxide. The most common form is a slender cone tapering to a point (the familiar icicle or carrot shape). This develops because calcite is deposited most abundantly where the water first is exposed to the air at the top of the stalactite. As the water flows down the stalactite, it approaches equilibrium with the air and deposits less and less calcite, causing the stalactite to taper.

Stalactites grow about one inch every century. The relative abundance of stalactites and stalagmites depends on the flow rates of the dripping water. When the flow rate is low, each drop can hang on the ceiling for a long time before succumbing to the dual action of gravity from below and another drop pushing from above. This enables more stalactite growth. When water flows more quickly, stalactites are fewer and smaller; however, stalagmites are larger and more numerous.

STALAGMITES

The dripstone formations that rise from cave floors are called stalagmites. They do not grow like plants, as was thought until the late 1700s, but are formed by much the same process as the stalactites that are their parents.

As water drops fall from the stalactites above, they carry excess carbon dioxide. When a drop strikes the ground, or the top of a stalagmite, gas escapes. This throws the water out of equilibrium; calcite precipitates in order to regain the balance. This precipitate forms a tiny mound-shaped deposit, and contributes to the growth of a stalagmite.

Stalagmites can grow straight up or in less regular fashion. Skinny, straight stalagmite formations are known as "broomsticks" for the item they resemble. When a stalactite and a stalagmite meet, a column is formed. A "stack of pancakes" forms when the drops splatter from a great height, depositing calcite over a greater diameter than for broomsticks.

Stalagmites are usually larger in diameter than the stalactites under which they form, and they are generally blunt, rounded, and smooth— not pointy. Stalagmites do not have central tubes.

DRAPERIES

Draperies are thin, translucent sheets of calcite than hang from cave ceilings. A drapery begins to form when a drop of water trickles down an inclined ceiling or other surface, depositing calcite. As other drops follow, the deposit gets larger, just like when a stalactite forms. Because the ceiling is slanted, the drop follows an irregular course. Therefore, the resulting deposit doesn't hang straight down, but forms an upside-down ledge on the ceiling. When enough material is deposited, a large sheet of calcite hangs from the cave ceiling, curved and folded to resemble draperies.

Variations in the water's mineral content may cause orange or brown streaks to alternate with lighter bands in the draperies. These impurities give the deposit a banded structure with a marked resemblance to bacon. Some draperies have serrated edges known as saw's teeth or fringe. Each tooth is a crystal.

This impressive stalagmite is at Lost World Caverns, West Virginia.

Draperies at Smoke Hole Caverns, West Virginia.

HELICTITES

If you want to make a name for yourself in the annals of geology, figure out exactly how helictites form. These twisting speleothems, sometimes known as "pigtails," stick out of cave walls, ceilings, floors, and other formations in a seemingly gravity-defying fashion. You can see many helictites at Skyline Caverns in Virginia.

These "eccentric stalactites," more than any other speleothems, have engendered all kinds of theories about their genesis. Condensa-

Pigtail-like helictites are plentiful at Lincoln Caverns, Pennfield, Pennsylvania.

tion of lime-containing vapor? Deposits on spider webs? Stone roots? A direct result of electrical energy or earthquakes? These are just some of the explanations put forth over the years.

Here's the current theory. Each helictite starts like a tiny stalactite with a narrow central canal. Water is forced under hydrostatic pressure from the cave wall along the helictite to the tip. The flow is so slow that a drop doesn't form as the water gets to the end of the helictite, therefore gravity does not affect the shape. Deposition takes place right around the hole in an irregular fashion, as might happen if you tried to blow water out a straw while holding your finger over the end.

Each new layer is cone-shaped. As new drops form, the crystals become slightly distorted and the structure is unstable, so a new cone never fits perfectly on the one it adheres to. This gives the helictite its spiral shape. In some caves groups of helictites point in the same direction, possibly due to air currents.

SHIELDS

Another speleothem related to the helictite is the shield. Shields (or "palettes") are paired round, flat disks of calcite formed by seeping water. Each shield is attached along its straight edge to the ceiling, wall, or floor of a cave. They project outward at various angles into the cave chamber.

Each shield consists of two parallel plates. They do not adhere to each other; water flows between them. The plates are separated by a fracture that extends from a joint in the limestone bedrock.

Water under pressure and containing dissolved calcium carbonate moves along the crack between the two plates out to the rim of the shield. Here calcite deposition occurs around the edges of the plates, and the shield slowly increases in diameter. Because hydrostatic pressure controls the water flow (as in helictites), shields may form at any angle on the walls, or may even grow upward from the floor.

Eventually, other speleothems begin to form on the shield. Shields are commonly ornamented with stalactites and draperies; helictites may form on their upper surfaces.

CAVE CORAL

These deposits are not made of coral at all, but are calcite speleothems. In some caves the walls are covered with cave coral, indicating that the cave was once flooded by calcite-saturated water.

A classic shield speleothem at Grand Caverns, Virginia.

These small, knobby clusters (also known as cave popcorn) occur in almost all caves. The generally smooth knobs are sometimes on branching stems. They often stick out several inches.

Cave coral forms most frequently along wall cracks or on silt deposits. Since dripping or flowing water is not present in those areas, cave coral most likely forms when water seeps out between the crystals. In some places, tubular stalactites hang from the terminal knobs of cave coral.

A speleothem that may form in a similar fashion to cave coral is the spherical stalactite. These are bulbous as opposed to conical; some are almost round. Massanutten Caverns in Virginia has excellent speci-

mens of these spherical stalactites. Like cave coral, water apparently
seeps through the stalactite crystals, depositing calcite on the surface.

Cave coral decorates the lower right of this wall at Massanutten Caverns, Virginia

RIMSTONE POOLS

The common steplike terraces on cave floors are known as rimstone dams. As water flows over rapids (or anything else that disturbs it), it is agitated, causing carbon dioxide gas to be given off. Calcite is deposited when the water loses its carbon dioxide, in an attempt to regain equilibrium. A low rim begins to form.

If water continues to flow into the pool, the pool will eventually overflow at the lowest point on its rim. As the overflow water goes over

These ridges—only inches high—trap water in rimstone pools at Howe Caverns, New York.

the dam, more evaporation and diffusion occur, hence more calcite is deposited. In this way the pool builds its own dam, also known as a "gour" barrier. The dam is kept level because water flows over the lowest place, depositing calcite until it is built up to the same height as the rest of the dam.

The dams usually occur in a series of curved steps enclosing pools; a waterfall effect is achieved as water flows over them from one pool to another. Rimstone dams vary widely in size; though generally only inches high, some are several feet tall.

ANTHODITES

Anthodites, nicknamed "stone flowers," are formed from a central core. Hairlike projections emerge from this core, forming petal-like crystal blooms.

Anthodites are composed of calcium carbonate, but in the form of aragonite, not calcite. Calcite and aragonite are known as polymorphs: they have the same chemical composition, but different atomic structures. Aragonite's unique structure and properties allow the beautiful flower-like anthodites to form. Skyline Caverns in Virginia is renowned for anthodites.

BOXWORK

You may see cracks in limestone caves that look almost like someone filled them with caulk. This checkerboard pattern of filled cracks is called boxwork, and it results when cracked limestone fills with waterborne calcite, cementing the layer.

Often, the calcite "caulk" that fills the cracks is not "smoothed out" with Mother Nature's trowel. Instead, calcite ribbons may stick out from the walls a little bit.

CAVE PEARLS

A unique type of calcite speleothem, the cave pearl or "oolite," forms in shallow pools of saturated water continually disturbed by dripping water. Calcite coats tiny pebbles, sand grains, or fragments of other speleothems on the bottom of the pool. The agitation of the water turns these grains and keeps them suspended. It also causes calcite to be released from the water and deposited around the grains in a complete shell. Concentric layers are deposited, creating a "pearl."

Anthodites at Skyline Caverns, Virginia.

Several pearls can sometimes be found in a "nest."

Cave pearls can be as small as a pinhead or as large as a grapefruit. Most of the smaller ones are nearly spherical; the larger ones are more irregular. When a pearl gets too heavy, it may sink and adhere to the bottom.

Unlike oyster pearls, cave pearls disintegrate when removed from the water.

OTHER CAVE DEPOSITS

Calcite speleothems, while the most eye-catching of cave deposits, are by no means the only deposits. Fossils, traces of ancient animals or plants, can often be found in limestone caves. These can be bones, tracks, imprints, or a mineral cast that replaced a plant or animal after its death.

The fallen blocks in cave passages are an inevitable result of breakdown, part of the cave's life cycle. Your guide will probably tell you that you don't have to worry about falling rocks. This is true because show caves are in the middle of their life cycle, when rockfall is uncommon.

Sand, silt, and clay in a cave can offer insight into its past. These mechanically deposited fills are as much a part of a cave's essence as the spellbinding calcite formations.

An example of boxwork at Howe Caverns, New York.

CHAPTER THREE

LIFE IN CAVES

A nimals that live in environments similar to caves and visit caves regularly are called troglophiles, "cave lovers." Animals that live in caves are called troglobites, "cave dwellers." Animals that regularly visit caves but cannot complete their life cycles underground are called trogloxenes, "cave guests."

Darkness is a disadvantage of the cave environment; however, caves have advantages for their inhabitants—notably, protection. Cave dwellers are safe from outside predators.

BATS

When people think "cave," they usually think "bat." And what they think is seldom complimentary to this small, fur-skinned, flying mammal. So let's set the record straight.

Bats are not blind. Bats are not dirty (in fact, they groom themselves fastidiously). Bats will not get caught in your hair. Some bats, like any species of wild mammal, have rabies, but instances of the disease are rare (less than 0.5% of bats). Even infected bats rarely bite. Family dogs are more dangerous to people than bats.

Bats are very small. Most species are only 2 to 4 inches long, with a wingspan about five times that. They feed at night and rest during the day by hanging upside-down in some cool, secluded spot like a cave.

Bats rely on sophisticated ultrasonic signals for their superb navigational ability. They generate high-pitched sounds, detect the echoes, and interpret the results. Bats use their echolocation mainly for catching insects in flight.

Fruit-eating bats are nature's most important seed-dispersing mammals. Bats are the only major predators of night-flying insects. Bat guano (excrement) is a major source of fertilizer. And there are no vampire bats in North America.

Caves in the middle Atlantic states do not have the vast numbers of bats found in southwestern caves. You may see a few bats, who most likely will be roosting. Think kindly about bats; they are important insectivores who have fallen victim to pollution, pesticides, and a shrinking habitat. The Endangered Species Protection Act mandates stiff fines and possible imprisonment for those who kill or disturb endangered bats or harm their habitat.

OTHER CAVE ANIMALS

Some crayfish, shrimp, and fish live their lives in caves. They are nearly colorless (sunlight is required for pigmentation), and totally blind. Some caves stock fish, such as trout, and provide light for them. These fish do not normally live in caves.

Cave crickets regularly visit caves to rest between their nightly excursions for food. Daddy longlegs often hibernate in caves. Several species of beetles inhabit caves. Bear skeletons indicate that these large mammals were frequent visitors to caves during the Ice Ages. Many hibernated underground. Other mammals, including raccoons, squirrels, and beavers, spend part of the day in caves but are not permanent residents.

If you see a furball like this, you're looking at a bat.

PLANT LIFE

Green plants cannot survive without light; it is an essential element of photosynthesis. If you see green plants or moss in commercial caves, it is because of the lights installed in the caves. It is not a natural phenomenon.

Ferns like these only grow in caves where artificial light is present.

CHAPTER FOUR

NEW YORK

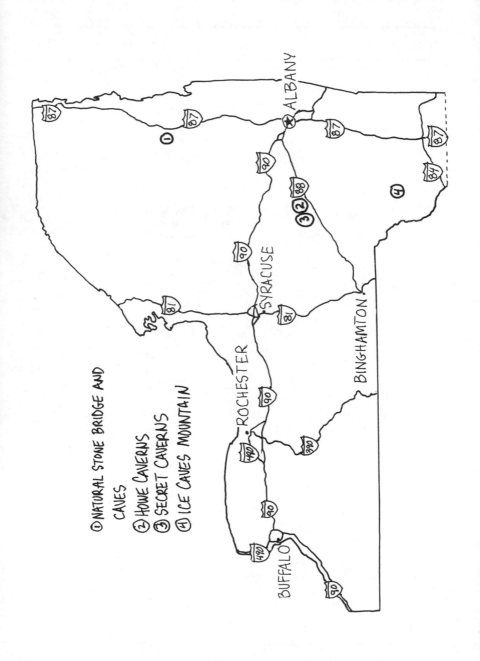

① NATURAL STONE BRIDGE AND
   CAVES
② HOWE CAVERNS
③ SECRET CAVERNS
④ ICE CAVES MOUNTAIN

Natural Stone Bridge and Caves

Pottersville, NY
Mailing Address: Stone Bridge Rd., Pottersville, NY 12860
Telephone: (518) 494-2283
Admission: adults, $6.50; ages 6-12, $4.00; senior citizens, $5.00; AAA members, adults, $5.50; ages 6-12, $3.50; pre-arranged group rates, adults, $5.00; ages 6-12, $3.00
Credit Cards: VISA, MasterCard, and American Express accepted for souvenir and mineral purchases with a $10.00 minimum purchase; not accepted for cave admission

Rock fall at the base of Natural Stone Bridge and Caves.

Personal Checks: not accepted
Season: May 24 to Labor Day, 8 a.m. to dusk; after Labor Day to October
    7, 9 a.m. to 6 p.m.
Maximum Tour Size: self-guided
Tour Duration: up to individuals, usually 1 to 2 hours
Wheelchair Accessible: no
Special Events: none
On-site Facilities: gift shop, rock and mineral shop, picnic areas, snack
    bar, jewelry shop, computer portrait center, fishing, rest rooms
Directions: Exit 26 off I-87; located 2 miles west of Route 9
Local Attractions: Barton's Garnet Mines, Frontier Town, Fort
    Ticonderoga, Schroon Lake, Lake George

As their mascot the bluebird proclaims, "Natural Stone Bridge and
Caves is something to chirp about."

Caves are only one part of the site's natural attractions. Cliffs,
potholes, waterfalls, even swimming exhibitions in July and August
make this a good place to explore at your own pace for an hour or two.

A store 2 miles down the road sells tickets, but don't come to a
screeching halt if you pass it by. You can also pay the admission fee at
the main building. One nice feature is that tickets are good for an
entire season; if you think you might return, get your ticket stamped
before you leave.

Some call it "walking," but others say that "hiking" is a better way to
describe a tour of Natural Stone Bridge. Walking sticks are offered to
those who want them, as long as you return them when you're done.
If you arrive wearing dress shoes, do yourself a favor and rent a pair of
sneakers from the office.

The first "attraction" you'll come to on your walk is an old sawmill
site, with an old beam and some stonework remaining. Walk on to
Meditation Isle for your initial glimpse of Natural Stone Bridge.

At Lookout Point you'll see marble rock over a billion years old, one
of the oldest rock formations in the country. And of course you'll want
to take pictures of the main attraction, Natural Stone Bridge.

Acidic water combined with the abrasive action of sand to create the
limestone caves in the area. Noisy Cave, named for the loud water
disappearing below, is the most impressive (although the lights that
turn on and off don't add much to the atmosphere). We tried to find
the "piggy-back turtles" that the sign hinted were made of rocks 4 feet
and 8 feet long, but alas, we never did see them.

The other caves are Echo Cave, where the exhibition swimmers start out, Garnet Cave, where they exit, and Lost Pool Cave. Lost Pool sometimes spouts a geyser at the left end. When we visited, the water was covered with foam (nicknamed Indian Soap). Supposedly, this is "natural pollution," the result of the effect of the water pressure combined with the normally acidic water attacking the limestone high in calcite. Maybe so, but it smelled pretty bad nonetheless.

On a recent visit we ran into Lydia Neubuck, who promoted the cave for thirty years following her high school graduation in 1941. Named "Cave Woman of the Year" in 1950, she occasionally visits from California to see the current owners (her sister and brother-in-law) and to check on the progress of Natural Stone Bridge. She is delighted that the attraction has been kept natural over the years.

Along with the usual selection of gift shop kitsch, Natural Stone Bridge and Caves has a fine mineral shop. It offers geode-cutting (pick your own and hope for the best) and an excellent selection of rocks, fossils, and minerals for sale.

Howe Caverns

Howes Cave, NY
Mailing Address: P.O. Box 107, Howes Cave, NY 12092
Telephone: (518) 296-8990 or (518) 296-8900
Admission: adults, $9.50; ages 7-12, $5.00; group rates available by prior
    arrangement
Credit Cards: VISA and MasterCard accepted in restaurant, motel, and
    gift shops; not accepted for cave admission
Personal Checks: New York only
Season: all year, 9 a.m. to 6 p.m.; closed Thanksgiving, Christmas Day,
    and New Year's Day
Maximum Tour Size: 40
Tour Duration: 1 hour and 20 minutes
Wheelchair Accessible: no
Special Events: American Cancer Society usually has a party here the
    Friday before Hallowe'en
On-site Facilities: gift and souvenir shops, fudge center, snack bar, rest
    rooms; from May to October, the restaurant and hotel are open
Directions: Exit 22 off I-88, follow signs
Local Attractions: Baseball Hall of Fame, Old Stone Fort, Secret
    Caverns

Howe Caverns is a lot more than a hole in the ground. In fact, it's one of America's most prominent show caves. Perhaps the best way to understand this attraction is to examine its rich history.

The caverns, formed millions of years ago by an underground river after the recession of the great glaciers, were opened to the public shortly after their discovery by local resident Lester Howe in 1842. (Conflicting explanations have Howe coming upon a hole during a fox hunt, or noticing that his cows liked to congregate over a hole from which cool air emanated.) An advertisement from Howe Caverns' early days evokes the flavor of time and place:

Draperies at Howe Caverns.

To Excursionists! Description of the cave: This is one of the most remarkable curiosities in the United States. For extent, beauty and variety of scenery, it is only equaled by the Mammoth Caves of Kentucky, with the advantages of being more convenient of access, and without danger.

This Cave is Lighted with gas as far as the Lake, a distance of about one mile....The air is pure and invigorating.

William S. McKean, Manager of Howe Caverns, published a booklet in 1885 that includes a description of the caves. Reading his words conjures an image of nineteenth-century adventurers following the procedure McKean describes for exploring this natural wonder:

Down a short flight of stairs from the office of the hotel, we find the dressing-rooms, and soon have on an underground suit, including thick boots, etc., and with an oscillating tin lamp rigged upon the end of a four-foot stick are ready for our underground journey.

Even in those days, guides delighted in treating visitors to TCD (total cave darkness). McKean describes "a stillness as of the grave" holding everything in silence as the guide tells his charges to blow out their lights, though they are far from daylight and have only a few matches on which to rely.

For various reasons, Howe Caverns was closed near the turn of the century and languished for decades. It was reopened to the public on Memorial Day in 1929.

Today, an imposing Tudor structure greets Howe Caverns' 200,000 annual visitors. This large building houses gift shops, a snack bar, and a lounge complete with stone fireplaces.

Of course, some things have changed since the days of underground suits and lanterns. An elevator now transports each tour 156 feet down into the cave (and, mercifully, brings everyone back up at the end). Formations nicknamed "Washington's Epaulet," "Aunt Chloe's Bonnet," and "Uncle Tom's Cabin" in the last century now have more modern monikers. A paved walkway runs the entire length of the tour area, and electric lights replace the lamps which once lit the colorful walls of the cave.

Tours are about one hour and twenty minutes, including a 1-mile walk and a quarter-mile boat ride on the Lake of Venus, a remnant of the ancient glacial ocean that once covered upstate New York. Impressive limestone walls and calcite formations include Balancing Rock, tobacco-leaf stalactites, Titan's Temple with its beautiful Chinese pagoda, and of course the Bridal Altar (over 245 weddings to date for couples who like 52-degree receptions).

Since Howe Caverns is so popular, your tour is likely to be crowded (there were forty people on ours). Don't hesitate to ask your guide to speak up or slow down if necessary. The staff is well-trained and articulate.

Quite a bit of memorabilia is on display in the lounge. Perhaps after touring the caverns in modern style you'll be a little bit wistful for the days when it was an Adventure with a capital "A."

Secret Caverns

Cobleskill, NY
Mailing Address: P.O. Box 88, Cobleskill, NY 12043
Telephone: (518) 296-8558
Admission: adults, $5.50; ages 6-11, $3.00; AAA members, adults, $5.00; ages 6-11, 2.50; groups of 10 or more people, $2.75 per ticket
Credit Cards: not accepted
Personal Checks: not accepted
Season: April 15 to April 30, 10 a.m. to 5 p.m.; May, June, and September, 9 a.m. to 6 p.m.; July and August, 9 a.m. to 8 p.m.; October, 10 a.m. to 5 p.m.
Maximum Tour Size: 20
Tour Duration: 45 minutes to 1 hour
Wheelchair Accessible: no
Special Events: none
On-site Facilities: gift shop, picnic area, park, rest rooms
Directions: I-88 to the Cobleskill Interchange, follow signs
Local Attractions: Baseball Hall of Fame, Old Stone Fort, Howe Caverns

Located five minutes' drive from Howe Caverns, Secret Caverns operates on a much less grand scale than its neighbor. This has its drawbacks, but it has some advantages, too. You won't find huge crowds at Secret, you won't have to wait in line, and you'll see a unique natural attraction that has a pleasantly homey atmosphere.

Secret's brochure does get in a subtle dig at Howe by saying that Secret's massive inner chambers have a unique beauty "so superior to other local caverns" that work was begun immediately to open Secret

Underground waterfall at Secret Caverns.

Caverns to the public after its discovery in 1928. As far as I'm concerned, Howe and Secret are both worth seeing.

The tour begins with a walk down 103 stairs into temperatures of 49-50 degrees. (Beware, the pathway may be muddy. Our guide swept the path in front of us, but we should have taken her cue and rolled up the legs of our pants.)

Stalactites, stalagmites, and flowstone formations sparkle as they take on shapes limited only by the imagination: Dinosaur's False Teeth, Claustrophobic's Corner, Lemon Squeeze, the Frozen Niagara, and Wonderland, among others.

The biggest attraction at Secret is the 100-foot underground waterfall thundering to the cavern floor. The air near the falls feels hotter and damper than the rest of the cavern because it's warmed and humidified by water from the surface. The rock in which Secret Caverns is found is from the lower Devonian Age (Coeyman's limestone) and the upper Silurian Age (Manlius limestone).

Although the caverns are hundreds of miles from the ocean, these rocks contain seashell and coral fossils, indicating that they are sedimentary rocks formed on the floor of an ancient sea that once covered most of North America.

The caverns in this area were formed largely during the last Ice Age, when waterfalls bored great holes (potholes) into the ground. Whenever these potholes were forced into a crevice, the water worked its way through the opening to create caverns.

For thousands of years, water saturated with minerals has been evaporating on the walls of the caverns, leaving calcite deposits to please the eye and stimulate the imagination.

The tour of Secret Caverns takes about 45 minutes, and, yes, you do have to walk back up the 103 steps. Our tour guide was pleasant and well-trained, making our tour of Secret Caverns an unpretentious yet informative one.

Ice Caves Mountain

Ellenville, NY
Telephone: (914)647-7989
Admission: adults, $6.00; ages 6-12, $4.00
Season: April 15 to June 14, 9 a.m. to 6 p.m.; June 15 to Labor Day, 9
    a.m. to dusk; after Labor Day to November 1, 9 a.m. to 6 p.m.
Maximum Tour Size: self-guided
Tour Duration: up to individuals, usually at least 2 hours
Wheelchair Access: no
Special Events: none
On-site Facilities: gift shop, rest rooms
Directions: 5 miles east of Ellenville on SR 52, then 3 miles north on
    road to Cragsmoor via signs

Ice Caves Mountain is a wooded area that holds a series of ice caves, hiking trails, and scenic overlooks. Designated a Registered Natural Landmark in 1967 by the National Park Service, the site is notable as a good place to see ice caves and explore the outdoors as well.

Ice caves form differently than limestone caves. In the cold winter

Ice Caves Mountain has a sense of humor.

months, bitter winter winds whip through the caves and cool the rock to below-freezing temperatures. In early spring, the mountaintop snow thaws and the melting water drips into the caves, wetting the cold rocks and forming ice. Wintertime, therefore, is not the best time of year to see formations in ice caves; spring and early summer are more likely to provide a spectacular array of crystal icicles.

In the summer months the ice melts slowly and often remains until early fall because of the insulating qualities of rock. Depending on annual variation, if you visit in late summer you may or may not actually see ice. (We went through the caves in late July and saw very little ice, although the temperature was quite cool.)

To explore Ice Caves Mountain, first stop at the shop and pick up a map. If you have a slightly warped sense of humor you may want to take advantage of a photo opportunity provided by a small billboard in front. A caveman (you supply the face) pulls his mate (ditto) by the hair under the caption, "I'm draggin' her to Ice Caves Mountain."

A written warning informs visitors of natural hazards that exist at the site, as they do for most outdoor activities: "Ice Caves Mountain National Landmark is a wilderness area with primitive roads and trails. Footing is sometimes poor, or changing conditions exist that require going slowly and using your best judgment...." Assuming you're not put off by this, go ahead and buy your ticket and pick up a map.

You can also borrow a tape to assist you on the self-guided tour. We found the recording informative and helpful, even though the narration was somewhat amateurish (lots of gulps, gasps, and microphone clicks). Also, don't be confused if the numbers on the educational signs don't match the numbers referenced on the tape as "stops."

You'll explore the mountain by car and on foot, so drive through the gate and stop as you please at the educational signs. At one point on your drive (Educational Sign No. 3), you'll be at the only point on Ice Caves Mountain where you can see both rocky layers of the ancient seabed simultaneously. On your right, weather and erosion have exposed dark, flaky shale that underlies the lighter-colored but very hard and brittle quartz conglomerate rock seen in the cliffs above. The dark rock resulted from layers of mud that hardened on the bottom of an ancient sea (360 million years ago). The quartz conglomerate was formed from sand deposits thirty million years later.

The next sign explains that a strange conglomerate of quartz seen in nearby cliffs was once an undersea mass of sandy pebbles. The pebbles congealed under pressure into 330-million-year-old solid rock. The cracks and crevices in this cemented quartz conglomerate were formed when the soft underlying shale was unable to support the massive weight of the mountaintop. Geologically, the ice caves were born in the deep crevices along the rock rim of Ice Caves Mountain.

As you drive along, you'll pass Lake Maratanza, the water supply for Ellenville. There are no fish because the rocky bottom does not grow plant life to give off enough oxygen to support them.

Ancient history of Ice Caves Mountain purports that about one million years ago mammoths roamed the area, as evidenced by their huge bones and remains found less than a mile away. More recent history is steeped in Indian lore (as told by white men), including the legend of Sam's Point, an overlook where you can see New York,

Pennsylvania, New Jersey, Connecticut, and Massachusetts.

The legend of Sam's Point has Trapper Sam cornered by an Indian war party in pioneer days. Supposedly, he escaped in a unique fashion which I won't reveal here. Suffice it to say that visitors should not try to duplicate Sam's feat.

The ice caves and rock formations, explored on foot, include the Rainbow Tunnel, Wall Street Canyon, and the Crystal Chasm. Be sure to "Duck your head. The rocks are much harder."

The self-guiding tour enables you to go at your own pace, but an average visit takes about three hours. Unfortunately, the fact that people can explore unaccompanied by guides also means that they can and do occasionally throw trash on the ground. Human nature aside, this masterpiece of nature is worth a stop for scenery lovers, camera enthusiasts, and fans of geology alike.

PENNSYLVANIA

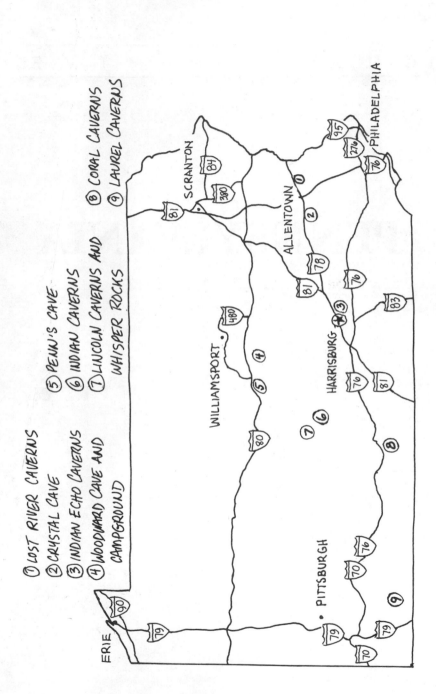

① LOST RIVER CAVERNS
② CRYSTAL CAVE
③ INDIAN ECHO CAVERNS
④ WOODWARD CAVE AND CAMPGROUND
⑤ PENN'S CAVE
⑥ INDIAN CAVERNS
⑦ LINCOLN CAVERNS AND WHISPER ROCKS
⑧ CORAL CAVERNS
⑨ LAUREL CAVERNS

Lost River Caverns

Hellertown, PA
Mailing Address: P.O. Box M, Durham St., Hellertown, PA 18055
Telephone: (215)838-8767
Admission: adults, $6; ages 6-12, $3.00; AAA members get 10% discount
Credit Cards: VISA, MasterCard, American Express, and Discover
Personal Checks: accepted with proper identification (valid driver's
    license)
Season: Memorial Day to Labor Day, 9 a.m. to 6 p.m.; rest of year, 9 a.m.
    to 5 p.m.; closed Thanksgiving Day, Christmas Day, and New
    Year's Day
Maximum Tour Size: 20 people
Tour Duration: 30 to 40 minutes
Wheelchair Accessible: yes, with assistance to negotiate eight steps
Special Events: none
On-site Facilities: gift shop, lapidary shop, museum, picnic area, rest
    rooms
Directions: from Quakertown, take Route 212 south to Route 412 east,
    follow signs to Lost River Caverns; from I-78, take Route 412 west,
    follow signs.
Local Attractions: Dorney Park

Discovered in 1883 while quarrying for limestone, Lost River Caverns became immediately popular among explorers. Here's how a writer from the *Springtown Weekly Times* described one of the early forays into the cave on July 17, 1886:

...at last find yourself in one of the grandest of apartments, the beauty of which puts to shame the mightiest efforts of human architects. The chamber is 230 feet long, it averages 26 feet in width and is probably 35 feet high. Within this cavern, every spot the eye rests upon it sees something new and wonderfully beautiful. Stalactites hang from every part of the roof. The north side is one mass of crystals, white as snow, and magnificently carved which reflects the light with blinding brilliancy. Beautiful statuary carved by the hand of nature fill the niches in the wall....Immense marble pillars run from the floor to the ceiling....The cave is an object of wonder and beauty and it is indescribable and to be fully appreciated it must be visited.

That should be enough to convince you. If not, perhaps you'll be

Impressive stalactite at Lost River Caverns.

intrigued by the mystery of the Lost River that carved the cave. After dye tests and human exploration, the origin and release of the river are still uncertain. In 1963 the river dried up, revealing a tunnel and a large room (65 feet long, 6 feet wide, and 12 feet high). Dubbed the Queen's Room, the only way to see it today is by looking at the picture in the lobby: the river is flowing again and the room is inaccessible.

Or maybe you'll want to see Oscar the flowstone turtle, a 300-pound ear of corn, or a cave orchid. Lost River Caverns claims to have at least one anthodite, although Skyline Caverns in Virginia says they're the only place where these speleothems form. It looked like an anthodite to us, but it's possible that the chemical composition or method of formation disqualifies it from this designation.

Opened in 1930 for tours, the cave has hosted numerous weddings and baptisms in its Crystal Chapel, decorated with beautiful flowstone formations. Tell your guests to wear long sleeves because the temperature is 52 degrees year round.

The building that covers the cave entrance also houses the Gilman Museum. The walls are covered with mooseheads, bear, deer, boar, and fish. Also inside is the Gilman Mineral and Lapidary Supply, with high-quality mineral specimens and crystals as well as lapidary equipment.

Crystal Cave

Kutztown, PA
Mailing Address: R.D. 3, Box 416, Kutztown, PA 19530
Telephone: (215)683-6765
Admission: adults, $6.00; ages 12 and under, $3.00
Season: March and April: every day, 9 a.m. to 5 p.m; May 1 to Memorial Day: Monday through Friday, 9 a.m. to 5 p.m.; weekends and holidays, 9 a.m. to 6 p.m.; Memorial Day to Labor Day: Monday through Friday, 9 a.m. to 6 p.m.; weekends and holidays, 9 a.m. to 7 p.m.; Labor Day through October 31: Monday through Friday, 9 a.m. to 5 p.m.; weekends and holidays, 9 a.m. to 6 p.m. November: Friday, Saturday, and Sunday only, 9 a.m. to 5 p.m.
Directions: follow signs off US 222, 2 miles to cave
Local Attractions: Roadside America, Blue Mountain and Reading Railroad, Village of Drehersville, Hawk Mountain Sanctuary, Pennsylvania Dutch Farm Museum, Pennsylvania Dutch Culture Center

"Ear of Corn" at Crystal Cave.

The oldest operating cave in Pennsylvania, Crystal Cave's modern history began in November, 1871, when two gentlemen working at a nearby quarry found an opening in the ground. Further probing indicated that they had discovered quite a large hole indeed. Along with some fellow adventurers and several coal oil lanterns, the two men returned to the cave the following day and were awed by the sight that met them: an underground fantasyland like nothing they had ever seen.

Soon after the cave's discovery, the 125 acres on which the cave is located were purchased by Samuel Kohler. Ever the entrepreneur,

Kohler began to admit the public (and charge admission) in 1873. The cave tours were an overnight success, so much so that Kohler built the cleverly named Cave Inn to accommodate visitors. Tourists would ride the Reading Railroad to nearby Virginville then complete the journey to Crystal Cave via horse-drawn carriages. In 1923 the land was purchased by a group of area investors who improved the cave and surrounding grounds.

Today's cave tours are preceded by (or followed with) a 10-minute educational slide presentation, "Inside the Earth." The narration, full of dramatic touches like "Back...back they went...," is nonetheless informative about the cave's history and geology. When we visited recently, the show was very well received by the audience (mainly tomahawk-toting children from a school group).

The cave entrance is at the top of a steep incline, made easier by the switchbacks that lead up the hill. The tour lasts about 35 minutes and is along concrete paths with railings throughout. Temperature year-round is 54 degrees. There are many dripstone and flowstone formations, including the Ear of Corn, Ice Cream Cone, Giant's Tooth, and Moldy Bacon, lit with colored and white lights. You'll also see Lake Inferior, which holds only 2 quarts of water. (It's nice to see a cave attraction poke fun at the size of one of its formations for a change.)

At the deepest part of the cave, guides turn off their flashlights to treat tourists to "total cave darkness," asking them to concentrate on their other senses and then pretending to abandon their charges with a promise to return after lunch.

Current animal life in the cave is counted at seven bats. Crystal Cave has hosted its share of celebrations, including baptisms and marriages.

There's also plenty to do outside the cave. Available to visitors at no charge are a playground, nature trail, Amish buggy, Indian tepees and totem poles, tree plantation and picnic park. In addition, Crystal Cave has a miniature golf course, a rock shop, an arcade, and a museum. Fast food and Pennsylvania Dutch specialties are available in the summer season. The gift shop provides items for those who want to take home souvenir T-shirts of the nearby towns of Intercourse, Blue Ball, and Virginville; if you are of a more serious bent, a comprehensive booklet about the cave's history is available. Information about lodging and nearby attractions is displayed in a case in front of the shop.

Indian Echo Caverns

Hummelstown, PA
Mailing Address: P.O. Box 188, Hummelstown, PA 17036 or P.O. Box
    745, Hershey, PA 17033
Telephone: (717)566-8131
Admission: adults, $6.00; ages 4-11, $3.00; senior citizens, $5.00; AAA
    members, adults, $5.00; ages 4-11, $2.50; group rates, adults,
    $4.50; ages 4-11, $2.25
Credit Cards: VISA and MasterCard
Personal Checks: not accepted

A wall of dripstone and flowstone decorates Indian Echo Caverns.

Season: Memorial Day to Labor Day, 9 a.m. to 6 p.m.; April, May,
      September, and October, 10 a.m. to 4 p.m.; March and November
      (weekends only) 10 a.m. to 4 p.m.
Maximum Tour Size: 28
Tour Duration: 45 minutes
Wheelchair Accessible: no
Special Events: none
On-site Facilities: gift shop, playground, Gem Mill Junction, picnic
      area, food cart, rest rooms
Directions: from US 322, take the Middletown/Hummelstown exit and
      follow signs mile to the caverns; from I-283 take the Vine Street
      Middletown/Hummelstown exit and follow the road to
      Hummelstown approximately 2 miles; from the Pennsylvania
      Turnpike, take Exit 19, follow I-283 east to the Vine Street
      Middletown/Hummelstown exit and follow the road to
      Hummelstown, approximately 2 miles; located 1 mile south of
      Hummelstown.
Local Attractions: Chocolate World and Hersheypark

No one knows exactly when Indian Echo Caverns was discovered; it's
possible that the Susquehannock Indians used the cave for food storage
and shelter, although there's no hard evidence. Maps of the cave date
back to 1753, cave carvings from the 1800s appear on the walls, and
smoke marks from hobos' fires are still visible today.

   One man, William Wilson, actually lived in Indian Echo Caverns
from 1802 until his death in 1821. Wilson's sister had been falsely
accused of murdering her twin sons. When the truth was discovered,
she was pardoned, but the reprieve came moments too late; she had
just been hanged for the crime. Her brother moved into Indian Echo
Caverns to escape the public and his memories. Visitors to Indian Echo
Caverns today don't come close to spending nineteen years inside the
cave like William Wilson: the average tour is about forty-five minutes.

   Besides the story of William Wilson, this cave has some other
interesting history. In 1919, three men from Hummelstown found in
the cave a box containing costume jewelry, a jar, and some coins (one
from Morocco dated 1288 and one from 1915 Turkey). Also in the box
was a formula, supposedly for making diamonds. Its origin still unex-
plained, the box is now on display in the gift shop.

   You'll get exercise before and after the tour, descending and climbing a flight of 84 steps to and from the entrance. We could have done
without the music blaring from a speaker over the entrance: it didn't

do much for putting us in the right frame of mind to see one of nature's wonders.

The cave itself is tastefully lit with white light throughout (except for a red flashing bulb that warns of a low ceiling). Formed by two rivers that ran through the cavern three to five million years ago, the cave encompasses two canyons and several large rooms. By far the biggest is the Indian Ballroom, 110 feet wide and 40 feet high. It was carved by a carbonic acid-containing whirlpool where the two rivers met. The Wall of Imagination in the Ballroom provides ample opportunity to see common objects personified in stone, as its name suggests.

Indian Echo boasts a wide variety of dripstone and flowstone formations. The oldest speleothem is the Tower of Babel column. Rare blue limestone adorns the ceiling in the Blue Room and the Rainbow Room. There's a flowstone Niagara Falls, and many small lakes.

If you can, try to visit Indian Echo Caverns in the off-season. Although tours leave every ten minutes so you won't have to wait long even on the busiest day, the ticket counter can be very crowded. Its current location inside the gift shop creates a difficult traffic pattern for shoppers and ticket buyers. More importantly, there is some doubling back on the tour, so visitors during busy times have to put up with some distractions: overhearing other guides, scrunching up against the walls to let other groups pass, and not being able to linger in front of the formations.

Nevertheless, the many stalactites, stalagmites, columns, flowstone formations, and lakes make Indian Echo worth seeing any time of year. Picnic facilities on the grounds accommodate up to 400 people. There's a playground for children. The gift shop carries a wide array of souvenirs, gifts, and Indian items, and you can even pan for gold at the Gem Mill Junction while you wait for your tour number to be called.

Woodward Cave and Campground

Woodward, PA
Mailing Address: State Route 45, Woodward, PA 16882
Telephone: (814) 349-9800
Admission: adults, $6; ages 5-12, $3.00; AAA discount from May 1 to June 30; group rates for 20 or more paid admissions
Season: March 1 to Friday before Memorial Day, 10 a.m. to 4 p.m.; Memorial Day weekend through Labor Day, 10 a.m. to 6 p.m.; after Labor Day through November 30, 10 a.m. to 4 p.m.; rest of year (weekends only), 10 a.m. to 4 p.m.

Directions: Woodward Cave is located on SR 45 at Woodward, 22 miles east of State College and 25 miles west of Lewisburg. From the east: turn off Routes 15, 147, or 104 onto Route 45 west. From the west: from State College, take Route 322 south to Route 45 east; from Bellefonte and Centre Hall, take Route 144 south to Route 45 east; from Lewistown, take Route 322 north onto Route 144 north to Route 45 east; from Route 192 turn south on Route 445; from I-80, use Exit 23 or 24 to Bellefonte from the west, and Exit 30 from the east, traveling south on Route 15 to Route 45 west

Young stalactites in Woodward Cave.

Local Attractions: Penn's Cave, Columbus Chapel and Boal Mansion
    Museum, Pennsylvania Military Museum

Woodward Cave, which bills itself as "the Big One," claims to be the
largest cavern in Pennsylvania. However, the National Speleological
Society gives Laurel Caverns that honor. Perhaps that designation
depends on the criteria used to define "large."

At any rate, Woodward has so much to offer that it doesn't need
any hyperbole. The tour, about one-half mile in length, covers five
large rooms on two different levels through well-lit, rolled gravel
passageways with many speleothems. At 48 degrees it's colder than
most commercial caves: air cooled by streams 50 feet underground is
pushed to the surface through only one entrance, the cave version of
"wind chill."

Woodward Cave is a water-formed cave in Ordovician limestone,
about 400 million years old. In more recent times, Seneca Indians
supposedly frequented the cave, taking shelter inside from severe
winter weather. Woodward's less desirable inhabitants also included a
band of robbers more than a century ago. The entrance was (and is)
big enough to accommodate men and horses. The cave was opened
commercially in 1926.

Stalactites and stalagmites are abundant at Woodward. One stalagmite, the Tower of Babel, is said to be the biggest in the state. It is 14
feet tall and weighs about 50 tons. At a mere 200 million years of age,
the formation is still growing. It's also unusual because it is freestanding
and can be viewed from all sides.

The Kneeling Camel is a dead (no longer growing) stalagmite that
was moved from a passageway into the Ballroom. This unusually shaped
formation once appeared in *Ripley's Believe It Or Not.*

Helictites, a rare calcium formation that resembles a pig's tail
hanging from the ceiling, are also present. Other formations include
the Lion's Head, Hanging Forest, Dragon's Den, Strip of Bacon, and
Liberty Bell.

Woodward is a fine place to see nature in action. Moisture droplets
hang from the flat ceilings throughout, depositing a little bit of calcium
before they plop to the ground. This creates a tiny stalactite that will
grow approximately one inch in a hundred years. (If you come back in
fifty years you might be able to see a perceptible change.) Stalactites
aren't fussy about where they begin: you can see some forming on the
wires that connect the light bulbs in the cave. The wiring was put in
during the 1930s and is scheduled for replacement soon.

Because Woodward is an "old" cave, fossils abound. Your guide will point out trilobites, a seashell fossil about 400 million years old. These are joined by none other than orthoponic cephalopods, your basic prehistoric squid.

Regulations demand that no one touch any formations in the cave. However, you can press your thumb into a wall of potter's clay, since speleothems don't form on the surface.

A few years ago, guides noticed thumb-sized holes forming on the cave walls. Usually, dripping water builds up stalagmites and does not erode the rock. After analysis, it was discovered that acid rain is the culprit, another indication of the sorry state of our environment and man's lack of respect for nature.

Woodward Cave is a significant habitat for bats (you remember that bats are helpful creatures who consume their body weight in insects each day in summer). The temperature is in the range in which bats can hibernate without freezing. Bats suffer from habitat loss and pollution, and from people who malign them with no reason. Woodward Cave management is interested in educating the public about bats and in keeping the cave environment bat-friendly.

The gift shop is small and does not have rocks for sale. Woodward Cave also offers a 19-acre camping area to accommodate tents and recreational vehicles.

Penn's Cave

Centre Hall, PA
Mailing Address: R.D. 2, Box 165A, Centre Hall, PA 16828
Telephone: (814) 364-1664
Admission: adults, $7.50; ages 3-12, $3.50; senior citizens, $6.50
Credit Cards: VISA and MasterCard
Personal Checks: not accepted
Season: February 15 to May 31, 9 a.m. to 5 p.m.; June 1 to August 31,
      9 a.m. to 7 p.m.; September 1 to November 30, 9 a.m. to 5 p.m.;
      December (weekends only), 11 a.m. to 4 p.m.; closed Thanksgiv-
      ing Day and Christmas Day
Maximum Tour Size: 25
Tour Duration: 50 to 55 minutes
Wheelchair Accessible: no
On-site Facilities: gift shop, picnic area, snack bar, airplane rides at
      Penn's Cave Airport, wildlife sanctuary, rest rooms

Directions: 5 miles east of Centre Hall on Route 192; from I-80, take
    Exit 24 south
Local Attractions: Penn State University, Woodward Cave, Indian Cav-
    erns, Boal Mansion, Pennsylvania Military Museum

It's a cave tour! It's a boat ride! It's Penn's Cave, the only all-water
commercial cave in the country. And if that's not enough for you,
Penn's Cave also has an inn (no longer in service), a wildlife refuge,
and an airstrip.

    The road to the site is well marked with signs, although the signs
themselves aren't marked well: sometimes "Penn's" has an apostrophe,

At Penn's Cave the tour is by boat.

and sometimes it doesn't. But if you're worried about directions, not punctuation, the signs are more than adequate.

Before reaching the gift shop/ticket office, you'll pass the old Penn's Cave Hotel. Built in 1885, the structure is classified on the National Register of Historic Places as "A fine example of late nineteenth century rural Pennsylvania architecture." Overnight guests were accommodated until 1919: Alexander Graham Bell was the most famous visitor.

The gift shop offers the usual fare plus a good selection of rocks. Hungry folks can chow down on a Cave Burger (if you're susceptible to motion sickness, you may want to wait until after the tour).

After buying your ticket, wander past some of the animals in the wildlife refuge. You'll see deer and pheasants, but these aren't nearly as impressive as Boomer the mountain lion. (Actually, Boomer is a Nittany lion—after all, you are in Penn State territory.) When we visited Penn's Cave, Boomer was swatting a tether ball, purring contentedly. Imagining his next meal of raw meat, no doubt.

Penn's Cave has erected several interpretive billboards that do a good job of explaining the cave's genesis and history. This enables visitors to absorb the information at their own pace and desired level of detail. One of the billboards recounts the touching legend of Penn's Cave:

In the early 18th century a Frenchman from Lancaster County, Malachi Boyer, explored the nearby wilderness, making friends with the Indians who lived in the forests. He met and fell in love with Nita-Nee, daughter of Chief O-Ko-Cho. They ran away when the Indians would not allow them to marry, but were captured and returned to O-Ko-Cho.

The Chief commanded his sons to throw Boyer into the water-filled cave. After a week, exhausted from trying to find a way out where the Indians would not see him, and vowing that his captors should not see him die, Boyer crawled into a far recess of the cavern and died.

And after all these years, those who have heard the legend declare that on still summer nights an unaccountable echo rings through the cavern which sounds like Nita-Nee, Nita-Nee.

If you need a little time to regain your composure after that melancholy tale, proceed slowly down the 48 steps to the boat launch. Our guide wiped the dewy gunwales for us before we entered the flat-bottomed craft. The boat is narrow, so expect to be knees-to-knees with the person across from you.

The water depth averages between three and five feet, and is fifteen feet at the deepest point. The water temperature is a chilly 38 degrees, so you will definitely not want to rock the boat.

One improvement to the tour would be the use of electric motors instead of the lawn-mower type, which are smelly, noisy, and distracting.

Penn's Cave is chock full of beautiful dripstone and flowstone formations, highlighted by the guide's flashlight: those suggesting the Statue of Liberty and a bunch of Chiquita bananas are easily recognized. Yellow, white, gray, and red minerals mixed with calcium carbonate color the formations in places, while lighting effects of red, green, turquoise, purple, and white transform others.

Have you ever seen a cave beaver? If you're lucky you will here. In reality it's just a regular beaver who pops into the cave for some rest and relaxation every once in a while.

After going the length of the cave, the boat exits and takes a turn around a somewhat scummy lake, made more interesting by a pair of mute swans. We had hoped that the boat would turn around before re-entering the cave, so that we could see what had been behind us on the way through, but unfortunately we went back in the same configuration, so we still couldn't see what we had missed going the other direction.

There are narrow passageways (The Strait of Gibraltar is the smallest) and low overhangs, so be sure to pay attention to your guide's instructions to duck. They come frequently on this unique fifty-minute tour.

Our guide earned extremely high marks for his "low bridge" warnings, geological knowledge, articulate speech, and good nature. In fact, this was the only cave tour we took where visitors gave the guide a round of applause.

Indian Caverns

Spruce Creek, PA
Mailing Address: Box 76, Spruce Creek, PA 16683
Telephone: (814) 632-7578
Admission: adults, $7.00; ages 6 to 12, $3.50; group rates available upon
        request
Credit Cards: not accepted
Personal Checks: accepted with two forms of identification
Season: April 1 to day before Memorial Day, 9 a.m. to 4 p.m.; Memorial

Day to Labor Day, 9 a.m. to 6 p.m; after Labor Day to November
30, 9 a.m. to 4 p.m.; rest of year (weekends only), 9 a.m. to 4 p.m.
Maximum Tour Size: 20 people
Tour Duration: 45 minutes
Wheelchair Accessible: no
Special Events: none
On-site Facilities: gift shop, picnic area, hiking trails, trout fishing, soda
machines, rest rooms
Directions: from the Pennsylvania Turnpike, take Fort Littleton Inter-
change 13, follow Route 522 north to Mt. Union, take Route 22
west to Water Street, then Route 45 to Indian Caverns; from I-80,

Indian Caverns features pictographs more than 400 years old.

Exit 20, take Route 970 south to Route 322 east to Philipsburg, then follow Route 350 via Bald Eagle to Indian Caverns; from I-80 Exit 23, take Route 220 south to Bald Eagle, then turn left on Route 350 south to Indian Caverns; from I-80, Exit 24, follow Route 26 south through State College to Pine Grove Mills, take Route 45 west directly to Indian Caverns; from I-80, Exit 25, follow Route 64 South to State College, continue on Route 26 to Pine Grove Mills, take Route 45 West directly to Indian Caverns; from US 322 at Boalsburg, take Route 45 west to Indian Caverns; from Pittsburgh, follow Route 22 east to Water Street, then take Route 45 East to Indian Caverns

Local Attractions: Horseshoe Curve, Bland's Park, Pennsylvania Military Museum, East Broad Top Railroad

Indian Caverns was used by Indians as a winter shelter, council chamber and burial ground more than 400 years ago. Behind that cave was another, separated from the first by only 14 feet of limestone.

The Indians didn't have dynamite at their disposal back then, but cave developers in 1929 did; the wall was blasted out to reveal Giant's Hall, the "cavern within the cavern."

Skeletal remains of American Indians, over 500 Indian relics and a tablet of Indian picture writing were unearthed in Indian Caverns. These relics and the tablet are on display in the Relic Room.

The mile-long tour begins in the Indian Grave Room, where most of the relics were found. Gravel paths make for easy walking in the comfortable 56-degree air. A narrow passage connects the main cavern with Giant's Hall, which contains the Frozen Niagara. Larger than a two-story building, this enormous sheet of flowstone is said to be the biggest formation of its type in Pennsylvania. It's estimated to be over a million years old.

The Jewel Room is where your guide will treat you to some different lighting effects. (In general the lighting in the cave is not great: you'll definitely need a flash for pictures even if you're using fast film.) This is also the place for total cave darkness, a chance to understand the phrase "afraid of the dark" on a little different level.

After doubling back through Giant's Hall, you'll pass through a room where outlaw David Lewis and his band were headquartered from 1816 to 1820. Next it's past the Devil's Bake Oven, which adds another possible wrinkle to the Hansel and Gretel story.

The Indian Council Room houses authentic pictographs. Our guide (whose patter through most of the tour was the "Say it, spell it, say it" format required in spelling bees) did a nice job of explaining the meaning of the writing: a tepee with open flaps means the body remains but the spirit is gone, signifying death. A quarter moon with three stars indicates that the person died in December. A turtle signifies the Mohawk Indians, and another symbol represents the Five Nations of the Iroquois.

The Relic Room didn't seem too impressive at first, just a couple of cases on the wall. But a closer look revealed an overwhelming number of artifacts: over 200 arrowheads, plus knives, scrapers, drills, paint cups, pipes, and chonqui stones that were used in a game of bowman's prowess.

The last room on the tour is the Grotto of the Wah Wah Taysee, or Star Room. Sparkles on the ceiling scared the Indians hundreds of years ago. And their fears were not misplaced: the pinpoints of light, still visible today, are caused by radium. (Don't worry, you'd have to stand there for years before suffering any ill effects.)

The Indian theme is played to the hilt: bathrooms are marked "Braves" and "Squaws."

One warning: if your vehicle is over 8 feet 2 inches high and a detour is in effect, you may have to go the long way round for adequate clearance. Your best bet is to call the caverns for alternate directions.

Lincoln Caverns and Whisper Rocks

Huntingdon, PA
Mailing Address: R.D. 1, Box 280, Huntingdon, PA 16652
Telephone: (814) 643-0268
Admission: adults (age 15 and older), $6.50; ages 5 to 14, $3.50; over age 65, $5.50; AAA members, adults, $5.50; ages 5 to 14, $3.00; groups with advance reservations qualify for reduced rates
Credit Cards: VISA and MasterCard accepted with $10.00 minimum purchase
Personal Checks: Pennsylvania checks only, with valid driver's license and major credit card
Season: March (weekends only), 9 a.m. to 5 p.m.; April and May, 9 a.m. to 5 p.m.; June to August, 9 a.m. to 7 p.m.; September and October, 9 a.m. to 5 p.m.; November and December (weekends only) 9 a.m. to 5 p.m.; other times by appointment
Maximum Tour Size: 15 people for regular tours, 20 for group tours, 30 for "Ghosts and Goblins" tour

Tour Duration: 1 hour
Wheelchair Accessible: most of the tour is not accessible, however, by
    advance arrangement the staff will show part of the caverns to
    wheelchair visitors
Special Events: "Ghosts and Goblins" tour on weekends in October
On-site Facilities: giftshop, nature trails, picnic pavillion, wooded pic-
    nic area, rest rooms
Directions: located on US 22, 3 miles west of Huntingdon
Local Attractions: Raystown Lake, Swigart Antique Car Museum, East
    Broad Top Steam Railroad, Bland's Park, Lakemont Amusement
    Park

Lincoln Caverns was discovered in 1930 by a road construction crew;
Whisper Rocks was found in 1941. Although the two are located on the
same site, they are not connected. Visitors tour one, then the other
through separate entrances for one admission fee. Touring both caves
takes about an hour.

The tour of Lincoln Caverns begins in the Mystery Room. It's not
known where the vast number of broken stalactites originated or how
they got into the tunnel.

Next, stroll down Pagoda Avenue with its colored lights to the
Pagoda Room. Eventually you end up at the Lobby Room, the first
room found by construction workers in 1930. It took seven men 13
months to prepare for the opening. The entrance used to be into this
room, but because of the traffic hazard (the door opened right onto
Route 22), it was moved in 1984. Today the concrete ceilings, bolts, and
beams detract somewhat from the "natural" state of the cave.

Lincoln Caverns claims to have the largest flowstone wall in Pennsylvania. In fact, they go one step further and say it's the biggest in the
eastern United States. Ninety feet wide and 40 feet high, the beautiful
wall of flowstone impressed us, whether or not it's the "biggest."

To get to Whisper Rocks after completing the Lincoln Caverns tour,
take a short climb up a steep hill. Smaller than its partner, the room
beneath the ridge is nonetheless spectacular. Called the Chapel Room,
it features thousands of stalactites, cave "popcorn," and sparkling
crystals. The National Speleological Society held their 1947 Easter
sunrise service here.

On the grounds are a Meditation Chapel, picnic area, and nature
trails. Your hosts, the Dunlavy family, have continued the tradition of
educational and entertaining guided tours, while striving to promote
cave conservation and protection.

One of the many columns in Lincoln Caverns.

Groups can arrange to see the presentation, "An Introduction to Speleology," free of charge at Lincoln Caverns or at their site. The combination of the guided tour, the slide presentation, and free supplementary materials supplied to teachers makes this program a complete cavern experience for school students. Lincoln Caverns publishes a brochure detailing the educational offerings and special rates for groups, available to teachers and youth group leaders upon request.

Dedicated to education, Lincoln Caverns' staff recently published *Pennsylvania's Caves and Caverns*. The 32-page activity book for children includes fun ways to learn about speleothems, cave life, and the importance of the cavern environment.

Coral Caverns

Mann's Choice, PA
Mailing Address: c/o Steve Hall, Mann's Choice, PA 15550
Telephone: (814)623-6882
Admission: adults, $6.00; ages 6-12, $3; group rates available with
       advance reservations
Credit Cards: not accepted
Checks: accepted
Season: Memorial Day weekend to Labor Day, 10 a.m. to 5:30 p.m.
Maximum number per tour: 30
Length of Tour: 45 minutes to 1 hour
Wheelchair Accessible: not yet, but working on it
Special Events: none
On-site Facilities: gift shop, soda machine, museum, rest rooms
Directions: from Bedford, take Route 30 west to Route 31, follow signs
Local Attractions: Shawnee State Park, Old Bedford Village, Skyline
       Drive of Pennsylvania, Fort Bedford, Bedford Springs, Gravity
       Hill

Touring Coral Caverns is like going through slices of time. It cuts through the middle of a Devonian coral reef, known as the only reef within a cave. Also significant is the towering "Fossil Wall," containing the fossilized remains of sea creatures buried for millions of years. This wall was once mud on the ocean floor. Over 100 species of coral are immortalized here, including stromatopora, a now-extinct coral that resembles lettuce or cabbage. It's hard to conceive of the sheer number of fossils that reveal themselves to those who take the time to look. Many helictites also festoon Coral Caverns.

The caverns were discovered in 1928 when workers quarrying lime-

Coral Caverns contains many fossils.

stone accidentally blasted through. Coral Caverns were opened to
public in 1932. Steve Hall bought the cave in 1981, and it became even
more special to him when he and his wife exchanged their wedding
vows in front of Pike's Peak, a large stalagmite.

The multilevel cave has formations like "Kissing Elephants," "Musical Stalactites," and the "Painted Desert," where cave coral has left a
bathtub ring. On the lower level you can see Devil's Pit, 135 feet deep.
One of the unusual parts of the tour is a demonstration of how black
light makes calcite crystals shine.

The shop has a wide selection of minerals. Museum cases hold fossils
and Civil War relics. Two suits of armor stand guard on the porch.

Laurel Caverns

Uniontown, PA
Mailing Address: R.D. 1, Box 10, Farmington, PA 15437
Telephone: (412) 329-5968
Admission: adults (18-64), $7.00; grades 7 to 12, $6.00; grades 1 to 6, $5.00;
    under age 6, free; over age 65, $6.00; miniature golf, $3.00; explor-
    atory, $10.00; AAA members get $1.00 off per ticket; groups (15 or
    more people from a recognized organization, with reservations)
    get $1.00 off regular tours and miniature golf, $2.00 off for
    exploratory; however, children under age 6 are charged $2.00

An ancient relic, not a modern explorer, at Laurel Caverns.

Credit Cards: not accepted

Personal Checks: not accepted

Season: May 1 to October 31, 9 a.m. to 5 p.m.; March, April, and November (weekends only), 9 a.m. to 5 p.m.

Maximum Tour Size: 22 adults

Tour Duration: 55 minutes

Wheelchair Accessible: no

Special Events: none

On-site Facilities: visitor's center, gift shop, indoor miniature golf, picnic area, indoor pavillion, campground, rest rooms

Directions: located on SR 2001 south of US 40, 8 miles east of Uniontown

Local Attractions: Fallingwater, Fort Necessity, Ohiopyle State Park

Located atop Chestnut Ridge in the beautiful Laurel Highlands, along a narrow road on which you're likely to see a deer or two, Laurel Caverns has much to offer. It is the largest natural cave north of the Mason-Dixon Line, listed in a 1988 National Speleological Society publication, *U.S. Caves Over 1 Mile.*

If you like numbers, the cave has approximately 192,000 square feet of floor space, or about 4.5 acres. There are 2.3 miles of passageways. The estimated volume of cave air exceeds 2,880,000 cubic feet. The surface property owned by Laurel Caverns covers 429 acres. The temperature is 52 degrees year round.

Laurel Caverns is a catacomb cave. It lacks the dripstone and flowstone formations found in some other caves, but instead it offers a labyrinth of long passageways. Very young by geological standards, the cave is "only" about 350 to 360 million years old.

One nice feature of this type of cave is that you can see many passageways off to the sides without having to walk through them. On the regular guided tour visitors walk about 2,400 feet but view about 4,000 feet of the cave.

Artifacts found near the cave's entrance indicate that Indians knew of its existence, as did the French during the time of the French and Indian War.

Laurel Caverns offers two types of guided tours: an hour-long guided tour and a 35-minute easy-to-walk tour.

And then there's The Exploratory.

For those who have never tried spelunking, or cave exploration, The Exploratory offers a way to "get your feet wet" without doing any hard-core gymnastics like rappelling or rope climbing. Laurel Caverns publishes recommended caving procedures with instructions on how to use the cave map. The publication describes caving as "kind of a mental challenge," which is a slight oversimplification of the matter since it ignores the physical side.

The trip is designed to be as safe as possible. Everyone is required to wear a hard hat, which can be borrowed for free. It's comforting that only 1 out of the 17,300 people who have gone on The Exploratory had to be rescued. Nonetheless, Laurel Caverns gives potential explorers a timetable describing what happens when someone is injured: an hour-by-hour catalog (in gruesome detail). "FOURTH HOUR: Rescue Team A finally reaches you, putting you in a Stokes Stretcher for the tortuous trip out." The explanation is designed to get you to think safe. Sure does the trick.

If you opt for the guided tour, you won't be disappointed. Our guide led us past the Grand Canyon, Devil's Staircase, and the Hall of the Mountain King. He described calcium carbonate dissolution as a "mild form of tooth decay," an analogy we could all understand. We saw a couple of bats, and our guide reminded us that they are "totally harmless unless you're an insect."

Laurel Caverns has done some clever marketing. A recent wedding there was reported in the local paper. They offer gift certificates. Picnic tables below the gift shop offer the possibility of having a birthday party in a cave.

Laurel Caverns also publishes a newsletter, and has a 16-page booklet available for those interested in a thorough explanation of the geology of the cave.

One of the improvements being made is a changeover to fluorescent lights. At the other end of the lighting spectrum is a proposal to host candlelight tours.

Unique among cave attractions is the really neat Laurel Caverns Miniature Cave Golf, which features a cave theme throughout. The indoor course passes an actual 1000-year-old Shawnee skeleton. Interpretive signs explain man's use of Laurel Caverns during the eighteenth and nineteenth centuries. The 12th hole is made more difficult with strobe lighting; the 13th green has voice-activated lighting. One hole has black light, and another hole must be crossed via a rope bridge over a deep cave chasm.

Outdoors, Laurel Caverns offers a surrey tram ride, weather permitting, Memorial Day through Labor Day (first ride at noon). The tram pauses en route to give visitors a panoramic view. On an exceptionally clear day you can see the US Steel building in Pittsburgh, fifty miles away.

The tram also stops at a fossil bed where visitors can look at fossils (brachiopods, crinoids, and trilobites, to name a few). Each person is allowed to keep one. On the ride back, the tram passes the remains of a French outpost believed to have been used to watch for the British in the French and Indian War.

Laurel Caverns has on-site camping with RV hookups. Camping and caving packages are available for groups.

CHAPTER SIX

MARYLAND

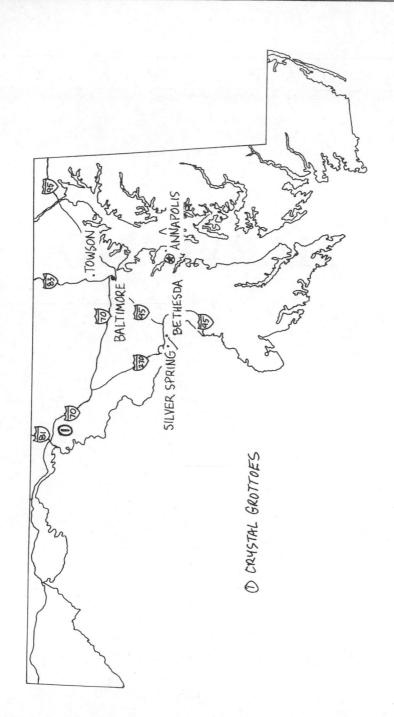

① CRYSTAL GROTTOES

Crystal Grottoes

Boonsboro, MD
Mailing Address: 19821 Sheperdstown Pike, Boonsboro, MD 21713
Telephone: (301)432-6336
Admission: adults, $7, ages 3-12, $3.50
Credit Cards: not accepted
Personal Checks: Maryland only
Season: March to November, 9 a.m. to 6 p.m.; December to February
    (weekends only), 11 a.m. to 5 p.m.
Maximum Tour Size: 15 people

Gleaming calcite at Crystal Grottoes.

Tour Duration: 30 minutes
Wheelchair Accessible: no
Special Events: none
On-site facilities: gift shop, picnic area, rest rooms
Directions: Route 70, follow signs.; Alt. 40 from Frederick; located on
    Route 1 in Boonsboro
Local Attractions: Antietam Battlefield, Washington Monument Park

In 1918 the road by Crystal Grottoes was begun. Blasting and drilling went on for two years for quarrying purposes, when much to the surprise of the crew, their drill bit simply fell out.

What it fell into was Crystal Grottoes, a 250-million-year-old cavern with many beautiful speleothems. Blasting was halted, and Crystal Grottoes was opened to the public in 1922.

It's thought that Crystal Grottoes was formed in the manner of a solution cave. Fissures in the limestone filled with mildly carbonated water from a sea that covered the Appalachian area. Intense tropical conditions prevailed. The seabed fell, dissolving the lime, then groundwater picked up calcium carbonate from vegetation. When the water permeated the rock deeply enough to hit the chamber, it dripped or evaporated, leaving mineral deposits behind. Until the happy accident with the drill bit, the cave was completely cut off from the outside: no rushing water from the surface came into or out of Crystal Grottoes.

Some of the formations are named after things they resemble: Father Time, the Snack Shop (you'll need hard teeth for this one), and the Blanket Room. Tour guides do a good job of altering the content of their presentations to suit the audience. The tour covers about one-seventh of a mile; the temperature is 54.6 degrees all year.

The chapel area has been the scene of two weddings. Legend has it that a girl's father forbade her to marry her suitor back in 1935. He told her he would not let her get married "anywhere on the face of this earth," so she decided to wed under the earth instead. In 1985 a couple from Hagerstown tied the knot dressed as Mohican Indians. Perhaps they used Indian "blankets" from the Blanket Room for their post-nuptial powwow.

CHAPTER SEVEN

WEST VIRGINIA

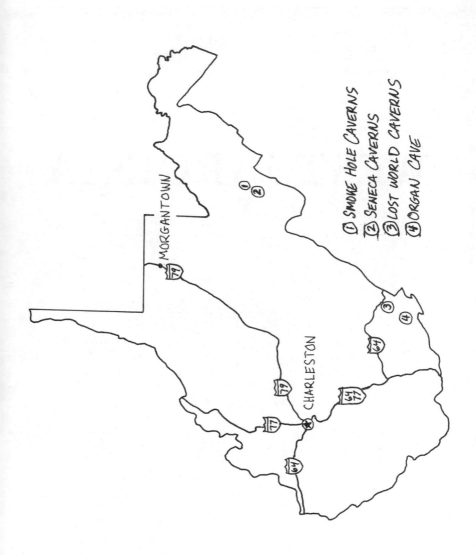

1 SMOKE HOLE CAVERNS
2 SENECA CAVERNS
3 LOST WORLD CAVERNS
4 ORGAN CAVE

MORGANTOWN

CHARLESTON

Smoke Hole Caverns

Seneca Rocks, WV
Mailing Address: Route 28 N., Seneca Rocks, WV 26884
Telephone: (304)257-4442, (304)257-1705, or (800)828-8478
Admission: adults, $6.00; ages 5-13, $3.50; group rates and AAA discount available
Credit Cards: VISA and MasterCard accepted
Personal Checks: West Virginia only
Season: Memorial Day to Labor Day, 8 a.m. to 7:30 p.m.; day after Labor Day to day before Memorial Day, 8 a.m. to 5 p.m.

These stalactites at Smoke Hole Caverns resemble a giant set of teeth.

Maximum Tour Size: 40 people
Tour Duration: 45 minutes
Wheelchair Accessible: some parts of the tour are accessible
Special Events: none
On-site Facilities: gift shop, wildlife museum, log motel, snack bar, rest
    rooms
Directions: located on Routes 28 and 55
Local Attractions: Dolly Sods, Seneca Rocks, Canaan Valley, Blackwater
    Falls, Spruce Knob, Seneca Caverns

Smoke Hole Caverns takes its name from the days when the Seneca
Indians used slow-burning wood fires to smoke venison and other wild
game. Early settlers saw endless clouds of smoke emanating from the
cave, hence the name.

Away from roads, and tucked away among boulders, Smoke Hole
Caverns made a perfect spot to store ammunition during the Civil War.
In fact, both sides took advantage of the location to do just that. Legend
has it that gold bars and coins, valued in the millions, were hidden in
the cavern walls, but they have not yet been found.

After the Civil War, the protected setting was used again, this time
by people who made corn whiskey moonshine. The cold, clear mountain stream within the caverns and various secluded rooms and crevices
made Smoke Hole an ideal spot for this activity, at least until the
"Revenooers" caught on. An abandoned still has been preserved for
display purposes.

Smoke Hole Caverns boasts many spectacular formations: the Crystal Cave Coral Pool, stocked with golden and rainbow trout from a
nearby hatchery; the World's Longest Ribbon or Bacon Stalactite (16
feet long and weighing in at 4 tons); and a sparkling Room of a Million
Stalactites, with a ceiling that towers 274 feet high. Smoke Hole Caverns
is turned on its side, with the "ceiling" now a wall.

The hour-long tour through passageways with a temperature of 56
degrees is interesting, but at prime time (summer months) the tour
groups can be as large as forty people. Smoke Hole has a large gift shop,
which also houses a snack bar and a wildlife museum.

Seneca Caverns

Riverton, WV
Mailing Address: P.O. Box 61, Riverton, WV 26814

Telephone: (304)567-2691
Admission: adults, $6.50; ages 6-11, $3.25; senior citizens, $5.85; groups
    with 15 or more paying adults, $5.00; ages 6-11, $2.50
Credit Cards: all major cards accepted
Personal Checks: West Virginia only
Season: April 1 to day before Memorial Day, 9 a.m. to 5 p.m.; Memorial
    Day to Labor Day, 8 a.m. to 7 p.m.; after Labor Day to October 31,
    9 a.m. to 5 p.m.
Maximum Tour Size: 50 people
Tour Duration: 40 minutes
Wheelchair Accessible: no
Special Events: none
On-site Facilities: gift shop, picnic area, snack bar, rest rooms
Directions: located on Route 9, 3 miles east of US 33 at Riverton
Local Attractions: Spruce Knob, Dolly Sods, Blackwater Falls, Seneca
    Rocks, Smoke Hole Caverns

Nestled in Pendleton County's panoramic Germany Valley, Seneca
Caverns are 2,500 feet above sea level and 165 feet below the surface
at the deepest point.

Evidence of Seneca Indian use is seen in the blackened walls of the
Grand Ballroom caused by heavy smoke from ceremonial and cooking
fires. This room was the actual wedding chapel of Princess Snow Bird,
the only daughter of Seneca Indian Chief Bald Eagle and his wife,
White Rock.

The 40-minute guided tour takes you past Mirror Lake, an underground waterpool that reflects the magnificent formations overhead.
You'll also visit the "Grand Ballroom," which is 60 feet long, 30 feet
wide, and as high as 70 feet in one area. It can hold several hundred
people and features a magnificent natural balcony on its back wall.

Seneca Caverns contains an abundance of snow white and creamy
flowstone laced with tawny colors. In several rooms you'll see flecks of
calcite crystals woven into the flowstone (called travertine), causing the
rocks to glisten as the light reflects off them.

Visitors' imaginations have come up with descriptive names for the
many formations: Niagara Falls Frozen Over, Princess Snow Bird,
Candy Mountain, Glacier Mountain, Dutch Oven, Fairyland, and Mirror Lake. Fairyland is a collection of rimstone, soda straw stalactites,
stalagmites and columns. As the brochure says with an interesting
grammatical innovation, special light effects make Fairyland a
"spellbounding" experience not to be missed.

Seneca Caverns has its own recycling program: formations that fell down or were torn down when the path was put in have been assembled in what's called the Cowboy's Antique Shop. This is the only place

Draperies hang from the walls of Seneca Caverns.

where rocks have been moved from one area to another: everything else has been left as nature intended.

Lost World Caverns

Lewisburg, WV
Mailing Address: P.O. Box 187, Lewisburg, WV 24901
Telephone: (304)645-6677, or (304)497-3192
Admission: adults, $6.00; ages 6-12, $3.00; AAA discount
Credit Cards: VISA and MasterCard accepted
Personal Checks: local checks only
Season: March 15 through end of May, 9 a.m. to 5 p.m.; June through Labor Day, 9 a.m. to 7 p.m.; after Labor Day to November 15, 9 a.m. to 5 p.m.
Directions: located 1 ½ miles north of Lewisburg. From I-64, take Exit 219. Proceed 1 ½ miles south to Arbuckle Lane, turn right for one block, then right on Fairview Road. Continue 1 ½ miles to sign
Local Attractions: North House Museum, Old Stone Church, the Greenbrier spa resort

All of the formations in Lost World Caverns are calcite, and all of them sparkle. Decorations of gray, rust, and buff punctuate the predominant white, giving a kaleidoscopic effect to this registered Natural Landmark.

Formations and speleothems here include soda straw stalactites, columns, draperies, bacon rind, shark teeth, rimstone pools, cave coral, and many other types of dripstone and flowstone speleothems. Looking around Lost World, it seems as if there are more formations per square foot than in any other cave.

One formation, the Snowy Chandelier, consists of pure white calcite. Estimated to weigh 30 tons, the Chandelier is one of the nation's largest stalactites. The many white formations surrounding the Chandelier have been nicknamed "snowballs."

The Goliath formation stands more than 40 feet tall and has a circumference of 25 feet. This column is a complex collection of stalactites, stalagmites, and draperies that have grown together for thousands of centuries.

Smaller than Goliath but still impressive, the Warclub stalagmite is estimated to be 500,000 years old, one of the world's oldest stalagmites.

At Lost World Caverns walls of speleothems are brightly lit.

Twenty-eight feet high, the Warclub has a base diameter of 2 feet and a top diameter of 4 feet.

Lost World was discovered in 1942 by speleologists from Virginia Polytechnic Institute. Ropes and ladders were used by these first explorers to drop 120 feet into a "dark, bottomless pit" through a maze of thick grapevines. The cave was named Grapevine Cave in honor of the vegetation that covered the first and only entrance. In 1970, a horizontal tunnel was dug into the main chamber, and Grapevine Cave was renamed Lost World Caverns.

Lost World was closed in 1978 for extensive entrance improvements and modifications. In the spring of 1981, the Caverns reopened with a new entrance tunnel, new walkways, and a new Reception Center and Gift Shop.

This wonder of nature remains at 51 degrees all year. The tour covers five-eighths of a mile and is unfortunately a bit rushed. Our group moved along too quickly for us to stop and read the interpretive signs. And since Lost World is so well-lit, it's a shame to have to rush through so many wonderful photo opportunities.

To explore the cave more fully, tours are available that cover the entire 3 miles. And if you really want to stick around and observe the natural beauty of Lost World Caverns, perhaps you'll consider trying to break the record of a stalagmite-sitter who perched on top of a formation in Lost World for fifteen days!

Organ Cave

Ronceverte, WV
Mailing Address: Rt. 2., Box 381, Ronceverte, WV 24970
Telephone: (304) 647-5551
Admission: adults, $5, ages 6-12, $2.50; AAA and AARP members get a
    10% discount; school and church groups of 10 people or more
    get a 20% discount
Credit Cards: not accepted
Personal Checks: accepted
Season: March to October, 9 a.m. to 7 p.m.; rest of year by appointment
Maximum Tour Size: 20
Tour Duration: 1 to 2 hours
Wheelchair Accessible: no
Special Events: Mother's Day 90-mile bike trek to benefit the American
    Lung Association; the trip goes from Cass to Organ Cave, con-
    cluding with a candlelight service and cave tour
On-Site Facilities: picnic area, playground, camping in the rough, gift
    shop, rest rooms
Directions: located on Route 63, 1 mile off Route 219, 5 miles off Route
    60, 7 miles off I-64 at Exit 175
Local Attractions: canoeing and white water rafting, trails for hiking
    and horseback riding, bike trails

A 40-foot-tall limestone formation that resembles a huge church organ gave Organ Cave and the surrounding community its name more than a century ago.

One of the many interesting passageways at Organ Cave.

One of the largest caves in the country (it's somewhere between the third and sixth largest, depending on who you talk to), Organ Cave is rich in history. It's suspected that the cave was explored as early as 1704, according to a date carved on the wall. It's known that Thomas Jefferson visited Organ Cave in 1791. Jefferson discovered and had removed a complete skeleton of a prehistoric animal, probably a cave sloth but possibly a dinosaur. The specimen is displayed in a Philadelphia museum.

Opened commercially in 1835, Organ Cave was the site of the stagecoach stop between White Sulphur Springs and Salt Sulphur Springs. It's said that women, undaunted by their cumbersome hoop skirts, joined the menfolk who explored the cave by crawling through it.

Organ Cave was a haven for Confederate forces during the Civil War. The cave was used by Lee's men for three purposes: for religious worship, as a retreat where they could rest, and most importantly as a source of saltpeter, one of the ingredients in gunpowder. The soldiers made ammunition here during the War Between the States.

Thirty-seven of the original 52 saltpeter hoppers remain, made from local woods and fastened together with wooden pegs. Wooden troughs were used to catch the nitrate-laden water solution, which was evaporated to provide gunpowder's main ingredient. The cave is dry enough to preserve the hoppers for at least another century.

Since 1926, Organ Cave has been in the family of the present owner, George Sively. Sively has fond memories of playing hide-and-seek in the cave as a child and what better place could one find for that game? Today, Sively gives tours, works in the store, and is happy to answer questions about Organ Cave or the surrounding area.

Organ Cave has many interesting passageways and formations along the well-lighted paths. The temperature remains at 55 degrees in all seasons, which starts to seem cold after a while since the tour is so long (ours was about an hour and a half). Some of the named formations are the Temple, Frozen Waterfalls, Majestic Organ, and naturally, a statue of Robert E. Lee. One bizarre manmade "formation" is a pair of mannequin legs sticking out of the rock. Beds of petrified sponge appear on the ceiling of the main passageway, along with thousands of fossils.

With over forty miles of passageways in total, Organ Cave has more to offer than you can see on the standard tour. To see the uncommercialized areas of the cave, you can participate in cave exploration with Venture Underground, a group that guides cave-exploring tours in West Virginia. Venture Underground offers full-day and half-day trips through Organ Cave. The tours do not require rigorous climbing or crawling, and the full-day tour comes with a subterranean picnic lunch. Contact Venture Underground at (304)645-6984.

CHAPTER EIGHT

VIRGINIA

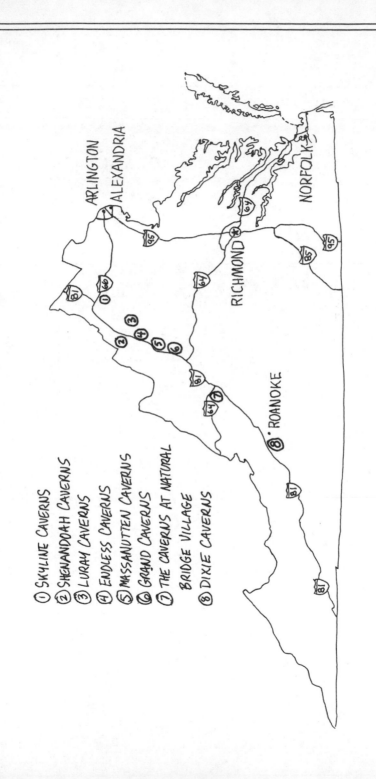

① SKYLINE CAVERNS
② SHENANDOAH CAVERNS
③ LURAY CAVERNS
④ ENDLESS CAVERNS
⑤ MASSANUTTEN CAVERNS
⑥ GRAND CAVERNS
⑦ THE CAVERNS AT NATURAL
   BRIDGE VILLAGE
⑧ DIXIE CAVERNS

ARLINGTON
ALEXANDRIA
NORFOLK
RICHMOND
ROANOKE

Skyline Caverns

Front Royal, VA
Mailing Address: P.O. Box 193, Front Royal, VA 22630
Telephone: (703)635-4545 or (703)635-4599
Admission: adults, $8.00; ages 6-12, $4.00; group rates for 10 to 20 people, adults, $6.00; ages 6-12, $3.00; senior citizens, $7.00; Armed Services personnel, $7.00; group rates for 21 or more people, adults, $5.00; ages 6-12, $3.00; school group discounts available
Credit Cards: VISA, MasterCard, and Discover accepted

Skyline Caverns is famous for its anthodites.

Personal Checks: accepted with identification

Season: March 15 to June 14, 9 a.m. to 5 p.m. weekdays, 9 a.m. to 6 p.m. weekends; June 15 to Labor Day, 9 a.m. to 6 p.m.; after Labor Day to November 14, 9 a.m. to 5 p.m. weekdays, 9 a.m. to 6 p.m. weekends; November 15 to March 14, 9 a.m. to 4 p.m.; extended hours available by advance request

Maximum Tour Size: 25 people

Tour Duration: 1 hour

Wheelchair Accessible: yes

Special Events: none

On-Site Facilities: gift shop, rock shop, fast food, country store, miniature train, picnic areas, rest rooms

Directions: follow signs from intersection of I-81 and I-66; located 1 mile south of Front Royal on US 340

Local Attractions: Skyline Drive, Confederate Museum, Dinosaur Land, Belle Boyd Cottage, Wayside Theatre, Oasis Vineyard

True, Skyline Caverns is decorated with many beautiful formations like the Painted Desert, Capitol Dome, Fairyland Lake, and the Grotto of the Nativity.

True, Skyline Caverns has three underground streams, one of which seems to flow in opposite directions at the same time.

And true, too, that Skyline Caverns was discovered in 1937 through inductive reasoning by Walter S. Amos, who analyzed local topography and announced that a cavern lay beneath the earth's surface (the only cavern known to have been discovered this way).

But Skyline Caverns' biggest claim to fame is not its wealth of dripstone, or its streams, or the way it was found. Skyline Caverns is exciting because it has anthodites.

Skyline is one of the few places in the world where anthodites, called "the orchids of the mineral kingdom," exist. Anthodites seem to defy gravity as their delicate white spines spread in all directions. Made of pure calcium carbonate, anthodites are crystals whose design is in the form of "rhombohedral cleavage." There is no generally accepted explanation for their formation, although one theory proposes that the vacuum that existed before the room was unsealed contributed to their development.

In any case, these "clinging flowers" are beautiful, even hidden behind chicken wire to protect them from the over-eager. They do look like flowers or like white sea urchins with many spines. The oldest anthodite is estimated to be 126,000 years old.

A sound and light show takes place away from the fragile anthodites at the 170,000-year-old Eagle. It's a presentation of the Creation, with background music supporting the narration of how "God was here...carving, molding...," that seems a bit overdramatic, but come to think of it, perhaps the beauty of caves does come from an unknown force.

The electrical wires at Skyline are extremely well-concealed, and the baskets that hold light bulbs are designed to prevent glare, a welcome consideration for photographers.

By the way, anthodites aren't the only thing unique to Skyline. The Caverns also boasts a species of shrimp beetle, *Pseudanophthalmus petrunkevitchi Valentine*, which lives only here.

For the little tykes or other train lovers, Skyline Caverns offers the Skyline Arrow above-ground. Built in one-fifth scale, this miniature train covers a half-mile around Horseshoe Curve, Apache Flats, Kissing Rock, and through Boot Hill Tunnel.

Shenandoah Caverns

New Market, VA
Mailing Address: Shenandoah Caverns, VA 22847-0200
Telephone: (703) 477-3115
Admission: adults, $7.00; ages 8-14, $3.50; AAA members, adults, $6.00; ages 8-14, $2.50; senior citizens, $6.00; group rates available on request
Credit Cards: VISA and MasterCard accepted
Personal Checks: not accepted
Season: April 15 to June 15, 9 a.m. to 5:15 p.m.; June 16 to Labor Day, 9 a.m. to 6:15 p.m.; after Labor Day to October 15, 9 a.m. to 5:15 p.m.; October 16 to April 14, 9 a.m. to 4:15 p.m.
Maximum Tour Size: 30 people
Tour Duration: 1 hour to 1 hour and 10 minutes
Wheelchair Accessible: approximately 70% of the tour is accessible to wheelchairs
Special Events: none
On-site Facilities: gift shop, picnic area, rest rooms
Directions: 1 mile west of I-81, Exit 68
Local Attractions: Shenandoah National Park, New Market Battlefield, Luray Caverns, Endless Caverns, Skyline Drive

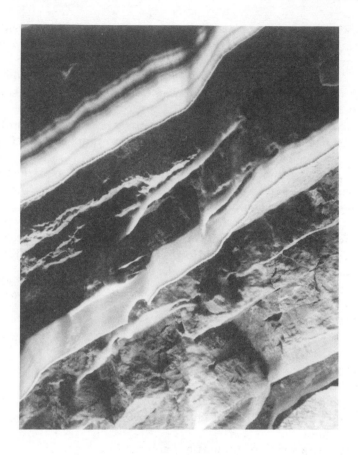

Bacon formation at Shenandoah Caverns.

The deepest show cave in Virginia, Shenandoah Caverns provides elevator service so that "only the sights are breathtaking." The hour-long tour follows paved passageways through temperatures that range from 48 to 56 degrees. Spacious rooms make it easy to see the many beautiful formations that adorn the cave.

Shenandoah Caverns' most famous moment was probably in June 1964, when its bacon formations were pictured in *National Geographic* Magazine. Minerals color these unusual dripstone speleothems to make them look like a giant (and harder) version of the breakfast side dish.

At the end of Bacon Hall, on the way to Grotto of the Gods, a suspended shelf displays numerous stalagmites. The Frost King's Palace is a large chamber thickly covered with flowstone and drapery stalactites, evidence of the large volume of water that passed through here at one time.

Shenandoah, which means "daughter of the stars," also has rare helictites and feathery-looking aragonite. Colorful travertine deposits are seen throughout. As is typical in caves, formations are named for objects they resemble. Shenandoah's Leaning Tower of Pisa, however, seems to be curiously devoid of windows. A balanced rock in the appropriately named Giant's Room weighs over 200 tons.

Luray Caverns

Luray, VA
Mailing Address: P.O. Box 748, Luray, VA 22835
Telephone: (703)743-6551
Admission: adults, $10.00; ages 7-14, $4.50. Discount for AAA members, AARP members, groups, and coupon-holders
Credit Cards: major credit cards are accepted in the gift shop but not for cave admission
Personal Checks: not accepted
Season: March 15 to June 14, 9 a.m. to 6 p.m.; June 15 to Labor Day, 9 a.m. to 7 p.m.; after Labor Day to October 31, 9 a.m. to 6 p.m.; November 1 to March 14, weekdays, 9 a.m. to 4 p.m.; Saturday and Sunday, 9 a.m. to 5 p.m.
Maximum Tour Size: 50 people
Tour Duration: 1 hour
Wheelchair Accessible: no
Special Events: none
On-site Facilities: gift shop, picnic area, fast food restaurant, rest rooms, gas station, motels, airport
Directions: Exit 67 off I-81, follow signs to caverns on US 211 by-pass west
Local Attractions: Shenandoah National Park, Skyline Drive, New Market Battlefield, Shenandoah Caverns, Endless Caverns

Luray Caverns is the most popular cave in the East, having hosted millions of visitors since its discovery in 1878. A travel center in the northern Shenandoah Valley, Luray is a full-service facility with a restaurant, gift shops, motels, recreational facilities, a campground, and an airport.

Luray Caverns' famous Stalacpipe Organ.

Tours into the beautiful Caverns leave every twenty minutes and last about an hour. All walkways are paved, and Luray is exceptionally well-lit. Even though there are several tours taking place simultaneously, distractions from other groups are minimal because of the way the tour is laid out. At 54 degrees and 87 percent humidity, the cave feels noticeably warmer than some others.

One of Luray's highlights is its one-of-a-kind Stalacpipe Organ. The inventor, Leland W. Sprinkle, "combined Man's Genius and the Hand of God" when he created this musical instrument. An engineer and accomplished organist, Sprinkle visited Luray for his son's fifth birthday in 1954. When he heard the clear tone emanating from a stalactite tapped with a mallet, Sprinkle envisioned a musical instrument that would incorporate a range of tones.

Stalactites tuned to concert pitch and accuracy are struck by electronically controlled, rubber-tipped plungers to produce music. The Great Stalacpipe Organ can be played from a large organ console or by automatic control (most tours will get the automatic version). The music is haunting and eerie, but retains its earthly (or below-earthly) rusticity, especially on some notes. "America the Beautiful" sounded like: La LA, la la, La LA, thunk thunk....

Profuse formations and natural colors decorate this large cavern. Flowstone and dripstone decorate passages, floors, and ceilings. The Giant Redwood, seven million years old, is 40 feet high with a circumference of 120 feet. Draperies form the Saracen's Tent, while white flowstone is nicknamed Titania's Wedding Veil.

A really nice thing Luray does is provide a special picture-taking area for people who do not have flash cameras. A large bank of lights is trained onto a formation-rich area, making it easy to get a good picture *sans* flash.

Because it's so big, Luray can seem impersonal. Our first contact with a Luray employee was an encounter with a surly woman who was not helpful in answering our questions about hours and parking. However, all of the other employees with whom we came in contact were eager to please and made up for the one bad apple.

The gift shop is large and well-stocked, as you might expect at such a sizable tourist attraction. If you're interested in the geologic aspects of the Luray Caverns, the book *Geology of Luray Caverns, Va.*, by John T. Hack and Leslie H. Durloo, Jr., is on sale in the shop. Foreign language guides are also available.

Included with the admission price is the entrance fee for the Historic Car and Carriage Caravan. The exhibit features antique coaches, carriages, cars, and costumes. Rudolph Valentino's 1925 Silver Ghost town car has an alligator-look body that's done with paint; a 1914 Locomobile Gentleman's Speedster sports a monocle windshield. Many prized vehicles are in the collection, which is well-maintained and interesting.

Not to be outdone by the underground Stalacpipe Organ, the Luray Singing Tower across the street from the main lodge contains a 47-bell carillon that is played regularly throughout the summer months. A carillon is a musical instrument consisting of at least 23 cast-bronze bells arranged in chromatic series and played from a keyboard. Each carillon bell sounds five pitches, including an unusual minor third which has a unique sound—it's an acquired taste. Concerts are free.

Endless Caverns

New Market, VA
Mailing Address: P.O. Box 859, New Market, VA 22844
Telephone: (703)740-3993, (703)896-CAVE, or (800)544-CAVE
Admission: the management recommends calling for prices; discounts
    are available to AAA and AARP members, military personnel, and
    groups
Credit Cards: VISA and MasterCard accepted with $10.00 minimum
    purchase
Personal Checks: not accepted
Season: March 15 to June 14, 9 a.m. to 5 p.m.; June 15 to Labor Day, 9
    a.m. to 7 p.m.; after Labor Day to November 14, 9 a.m. to 5 p.m.;
    November 15 to March 14, 9 a.m. to 4 p.m.
Maximum Tour Size: varies
Tour Duration: 1 hour and 15 minutes
Wheelchair Accessible: no
Special Events: Hallowe'en tours and Christmas open house
On-site Facilities: rock and gift shop, playground, picnic area, camp-
    ground, rest rooms
Directions: Exit 66 or 67 off I-81. From Exit 66, north on US 11 for 3
    miles; from Exit 67, south on US 11 for 3 miles
Local Attractions: Luray Caverns, Shenandoah Caverns, New Market
    Battlefield, Skyline Drive

Endless Caverns was discovered in 1879 by two boys and their dog on
a rabbit-hunting expedition. When the rabbit disappeared under a
boulder, the boys moved the rock and found a chasm. Explorations
began and have continued since then, though no end has been found
to the winding passageways. It was opened to the public in 1920.

   The walking distance is nine-tenths of a mile, with some backtracking
and a few slippery spots. If your tour group is large, you may want to wait
for the next one: since many of the passages are narrow, only the people
closest to the guide can hear or see what's being pointed out.

   Highlights of the tour include the Grand Canyon, Weeping Willow
Way, Oriental Palace, Mitten Room, and Snowdrift. In the Cathedral
Room, lighting effects are used to simulate a sunrise as strains of Liszt
fill the air.

   The gift shop has a wide selection of souvenirs. There is also an
excellent selection of brochures for local attractions and for other
caves nationwide.

Glistening dripstone at Endless Caverns.

Massanutten Caverns

Keezletown, VA
Mailing Address: Keezletown, VA 22832
Telephone: (703) 269-6555
Admission: adults, $8.50; ages 6-12, $4.00; groups of 15 or more people, adults, $4.00; ages 6-12, $2.00
Credit Cards: not accepted
Personal Checks: not accepted
Season: April 1 to October 31, noon to 5 p.m.; November 1 to March 31 (weekends only), noon to 4:30 p.m.

Maximum Tour Size: 20 people
Tour Duration: 1 hour 15 minutes to 1 hour 30 minutes
Wheelchair Accessible: two rooms are accessible
Special Events: none
On-site facilities: none
Directions: 2 miles south of US 33, mile northeast of Keezletown, just
        east of Harrisonburg off I-81
Local Attractions: Skyline Drive, New Market Battlefield

The experience of visiting Massanutten Caverns cannot be separated
from the experience of meeting its owner, Bradford Cobb.

Beautiful formations are seen whichever way you look at Massanutten Caverns.

After requesting information about Massanutten, I received a hand-written letter from Cobb, along with a brochure:

I hope that this brochure meets your expectations. The Caverns has no steps but many formations. Unless economic conditions change drastically, I expect to be running the tours without any other guides....

As the tour takes over an hour's time, this may be too long for some people. However, if you like caves, this can be quite satisfactory.

Some visitors do not want to be rushed. Actually, the tour is one of the shortest distances in the state so it is not tiring.

I hope that you will come.

We did, and found Massanutten full of surprises. First came a sinking feeling that it might be closed, since the parking area was weed-choked and there were no signs posted and no visible office. But we noticed a man sitting in a pickup truck in the lot, so we approached him. Lo and behold it was Bradford Cobb, chief cook and bottle washer of Massanutten Caverns. As Cobb puts it, "Either I own the cave or the cave owns me."

After having difficulty finding tour guides ("The kids want money like they can get in DC."), Cobb began giving the tours himself in 1988. An unfortunate series of physical ailments, including a stroke and cataracts, may have slowed his step a little, but they have certainly not stopped him nor dampened his enthusiasm for the beautiful cavern at which he plays host.

The romantic-sounding name of "Massanutten" means something a bit more mundane: "Place where potatoes are planted." Cobb describes the cave as two caves: the outside one for strength and the inside one for show.

And what a show! The shallowest cave in Virginia has thousands of speleothems. The nicknames for formations are similar to those all caves use: Wonderland, the Chinese Temple, Icicle Avenue. But a list of these formations does not prepare the visitor for the vast number and sparkling beauty found in Massanutten. The ceiling is flat throughout, providing a perfect platform on which stalactites develop. Aragonite, ribbonstone, draperies, and embedded geodes embellish the walls, floors, and ceilings. New wiring provides fine illumination for many areas of formations.

The tour is indeed long (almost an hour and a half). The most strenuous part is getting up a moderate hill to the cave entrance. The cave itself has no steps so it's an easy walk. Wheelchair users can tour two rooms at Massanutten with the help of traveling companions to get them through narrow "doorways." (Wheelchairs are not permitted where they could damage the cave.)

There is no shop at the cave, and no other facilities. Because Massanutten is essentially a one-man operation, it is prudent to call ahead if you plan to visit this spectacular subterranean wonder.

Grand Caverns

Grottoes, VA
Mailing Address: P.O. Box 478, Grottoes, VA 24441
Telephone: (703) 249-5705
Admission: adults, $8.00; ages 6-12, $5.00; senior citizens $6.00; AAA
    members $6.00; group rates (15 or more people), adults, $6.00;
    ages 6-12, $4.00.
Credit Cards: VISA and MasterCard accepted
Personal Checks: Virgina only, with proper identification
Season: March (Saturday and Sunday only), 9 a.m. to 5 p.m.; daily, April
    to October, 9 a.m. to 5 p.m.; open November to February to
    groups by reservation
Maximum Tour Size: 35 people
Tour Duration: 1 hour
Wheelchair Accessible: no
Special Events: haunted Hallowe'en cave
On-site Facilities: gift shop, swimming pool, miniature golf, tennis,
    picnic areas, rest rooms
Directions: Exit 60 off I-81, seven miles east on SR 256
Local Attractions: Natural Chimneys Regional Park, Skyline Drive, Blue
    Ridge Parkway, New Market Battlefield

Located within Grand Caverns Regional Park, this designated Natural Landmark is an imposing example of geological forces.

The atmosphere at Grand Caverns is congenial yet refined. The spacious lot below the entrance provides ample parking spaces and is surrounded by the grassy picnic areas of the regional park. (Mildly disconcerting was the loud music broadcast from overhead speakers.) The gift shop is more restrained than most, with wide aisles and open spaces. There are some souvenir tomtoms and baskets for sale, but the shop also offers a nice selection of rocks and some good books. Artifacts found in the cave are displayed and clearly labeled in a case near where the tour groups enter the cave.

A compound formation at Grand Caverns.

Known for its spacious rooms and numerous shield formations, Grand Caverns also boasts "vertical ceilings" going east to west, implying that the cave was somehow turned on its side. Visitors walk 1 mile on gravel paths in 53-degree air past Cleopatra's Throne (colored gray with magnesium), the Persian Palace, and Dante's Inferno. Hundreds of shield formations, including Ajax's Shield, Angel Wing Shield, and the Oyster Shell Shield, make this cave a showcase for this type of speleothem.

The cave was discovered in 1804, and opened to the public two years later, making it America's oldest show cave. Thomas Jefferson visited the Caverns, riding over from nearby Monticello on horseback. In

Jefferson Hall is what's claimed to be the second-largest stalagmite in the United States. The formation is 80 feet in circumference and 40 feet high. Called the Capitol Building, it is estimated to be 130 million years old.

Until the 1830s, dances were frequently held in the Grand Ballroom. The Civil War brought a less pleasant use for the cave, when Confederate General "Stonewall" Jackson quartered his troops there.

Grand Caverns was the first cave to have electric lights, installed in 1889 by Westinghouse (the company still gets a free plug by tour guides). Of course, the lights are turned out briefly during the tour, giving visitors a chance to experience total cave darkness.

Although our tour group was large (about 25 people), the large rooms made it possible for everyone to hear the guide and see what's being pointed out. Colored lights are used only in a few carefully chosen places, letting the natural beauty of the formations shine through.

The Caverns at Natural Bridge Village

Natural Bridge, VA
Mailing Address: P.O. Box 57, Natural Bridge, VA 24578
Telephone: (703) 291-2121; toll-free in Virginia, (800) 533-1410; toll-free outside Virginia, (800) 336-5727
Admission: adults, $7.00; ages 6-15, $3.50; senior citizens, AAA members, and groups, adults, $6.00; ages 6-15, $2.50.
Credit Cards: VISA, MasterCard, American Express, and Discover accepted
Personal Checks: accepted for group tours by advance arrangement
Season: January to March, 10 a.m. to 4 p.m.; April and May, 10 a.m. to 5 p.m., June to August, 10 a.m. to 7 p.m., September and October, 10 a.m. to 5 p.m., November and December, 10 a.m. to 4 p.m.
Maximum Tour Size: 20 people
Tour Duration: 40 minutes
Wheelchair Accessible: no
Special Events: wild cave tour, a 3- to 4-hour guided tour through undeveloped portions of the cave; fee, $20.00; advance reservations required
On-site facilities: Natural Bridge and Wax Museum attractions, including gift shops, restaurants, lodging, picnic facilities, swimming, tennis courts, fudge and cookie shop, golf course, rest rooms
Directions: from I-81 southbound, take Exit 50 onto US 11 for 3 miles;

from I-81 northbound, take Exit 49 onto US 11 for 2 miles;
located approximately 250 yards from the junction of US 11 and
Rt. 130
Local Attractions: Natural Bridge Zoo, Blue Ridge Parkway, historic city
of Lexington

As its name suggests, there is indeed a natural bridge here, along with
caverns. The bridge is an imposing geological structure 215 feet high
and 90 feet long, historically renowned because it was owned by
Thomas Jefferson and surveyed for Lord Fairfax by George Washington, whose carved initials are still visible.

Hanging draperies line the walls at Natural Bridge Caverns.

The story associated with the caverns is of a more spooky sort. Legend has it that in 1891 some of the locals were getting the caverns ready for the public when they broke through a solid rock wall into a room with a hundred-foot ceiling. All of a sudden, an unnatural hush fell over the workers, during which they heard a woman's voice moaning softly, then louder. The men turned tail, abandoning two years' worth of work. In 1978, when the caverns were finally developed, their tools were just as they had left them almost a century before. Supposedly, the "moaning" sound has been heard four times since the caverns were opened to the public.

If you can put your fear of ghosts aside, the Natural Bridge Caverns is worth a trip. Still active, the cave is approximately ten million years old with interesting speleothems, though it is not as formation-rich as some other Virginia caves. A plant-lined entrance and wide concrete sidewalk make the transition between the earthly and below-earthly worlds.

The Colossal Dome Room contains one of the largest masses of flowstone in the eastern United States. The dome's base is called a "compound structure," which consists of one or more stalagmites, roof fragments, and fallen stalactites that were then covered by flowstone. The Dome has become a column, connected to the ceiling by stalactites that touch its base.

Between the Colossal Dome Room and Mirror Lake is a 3-inch-thick layer of chert (also called flint) formed when the enclosing rocks were being deposited in the sea. This hard rock, a form of quartz, was used by the Indians for arrowheads.

After Mirror Lake and the Waterfall Room, visitors reach the Wishing Well Room, home of some of the loveliest formations in the Caverns. About 350 feet below the earth's surface, the room is resplendent with stalactites and helictites. Helictites grow downward from the ceiling like stalactites, but unlike those icicle-shaped speleothems, they curl and twist like a pig's tail. A widely accepted theory is that these formations begin as "soda straws" that are then clogged by some sort of mineral, forcing the water out the side of the straw rather than out the bottom. Capillary action may also contribute to their unique shape.

It is the Canyon Room in which the eerie sound was heard back in 1891. Don't be too scared to note the high ceiling and narrow passage in this area. The canyon shape is due to erosion along an area of heavy fracturing.

The tour lasts approximately forty minutes and is somewhat strenuous. The 54-degree temperature is refreshing and pleasant, and so is the fact that tours are limited to no more than twenty people.

Notable is an excellent book, *Natural Bridge and Natural Bridge Caverns*, which contains a thorough yet understandable explanation of the origin of caves. The book ($3.95) also provides an interpretive guide to the Natural Bridge Caverns tour.

While in the area, visit the Natural Bridge from 7 a.m. until dusk year-round. After dark, the "Drama of Creation" is presented outdoors (in season). The detailed features of the bridge are highlighted, with narration, accompanying organ, and mixed chorus, in a light show depicting the seven days of Creation.

Dixie Caverns

Salem, VA
Mailing Address: 6020 Oriole La., Roanoke, VA 24018
Telephone: (703)380-2085
Admission: adults, $4.50; ages 5-12, $2.50; for groups of ten or more, adults, $3.00; ages 5-12, $1.50. No charge for teachers and bus drivers with groups
Credit Cards: VISA, MasterCard, American Express and Discover
Personal Checks: Virginia only
Season: May to September, 9 a.m. to 7 p.m.; October to April, Monday to Friday, 9:30 a.m. to 6 p.m.; weekends, 9 a.m. to 7 p.m.; closed Christmas Day.
Maximum Tour Size: 25 people
Tour Duration: 45 minutes
Wheelchair Accessible: no
Special Events: haunted Hallowe'en cave
On-site facilities: pottery shop, Christmas shop, rock and mineral shop, picnic area, campground, rest rooms
Directions: located on US 11 and US 460, two minutes off I-81 at Exit 39, southwest of Roanoke
Local Attractions: Blue Ridge Parkway, Transportation Museum, Mill Mountain Children's Zoo, Center-in-the-Square (Roanoke)

Located on the Salem fault line in southwest Virginia, Dixie Caverns is unusual because the initial part of the tour goes up into a mountain rather than down.

The first stop on the one-hour tour is the Cathedral Room, over 200 feet in length and width, and more than 160 feet high. After passing the Turkey Wing (affectionately known as "George") and the Magic

Pool of water receives drops from above at Dixie Caverns.

Mirror, you'll see an active formation called the Wedding Bell. This 57-ton, bell-shaped speleothem has united many couples in "wetted" bliss, courtesy of water dripping from it as it grows ever so slowly.

Like most Virginia caves, Dixie Caverns was used for saltpeter mining at one time. It has also been the site of square dances and other gatherings, and may have been used in bygone days by Shawnee Indians as a source of clay.

Dixie Caverns is graced with many speleothems, including draperies, rimstone, and flowstone. The largest flowstone formation in the cave is the Golden Cascade.

Our guide, chairman of the local National Speleological Society

6 0 04 2

grotto, had more than a passing interest in geology and made the tour very meaningful. He pointed out formations like the Leaning Tower and the Frozen Waterfall, but also explained the genesis of the various formations and sounded like he knew the subject matter.

The Dixie Caverns staff is in the process of examining their environment for several reasons. For one thing, they are trying to find a connection to New Dixie, an extensive underground system nearby. Also, minerals and chemicals are being studied in order to assess pollution in the area.

For the adventurous, Halloween finds the cave cloaked in haunted garb. Exploratory caving, or wild caving, is available and can provide a good first spelunking experience for people who do not want to invest in a lot of expensive equipment before giving the hobby a try.

Shoppers are not forgotten at the Dixie Caverns Pottery Shop, which in fact gets more hype than the caverns do in the Dixie Caverns brochure. Accurately described as "a major buying feast with thousands and thousands of pottery items, cement items, candles, hurricane shades, glassware, baskets, gifts, gifts and more gifts," the store also has one aisle of rocks and minerals for collectors.

Complete camping facilities are available on site at reasonable rates. Those with recreational vehicles are advised to use their own bathrooms, though: the bathhouse did not pass my cleanliness test.

GLOSSARY

Anthodite: A flower-like formation formed by seepage through a central canal and deposition on the tip. Anthodites are made of aragonite or calcite; the needle-like protrusions resemble the spines of a sea urchin. Also known as "cave orchids."

Aragonite: A mineral composed of calcium carbonate (calcium, carbon, and oxygen), aragonite has the same composition as calcite but with a different arrangement of atoms, so its crystal form differs from that of calcite. It occurs as transparent, sharp-pointed crystals that sometimes coat stalactites, and can also appear as coarse fibrous or columnar masses. Aragonite is more soluble than calcite.

Arthropods: Animals with jointed legs and exoskeletons (hard external skeletons), including insects, arachnids, crustaceans, and other animals found in caves.

Bacon: A drapery formation with alternating darker and lighter bands, resulting from variations in the mineral content of the dripping water that forms it. When lit, these formations resemble bacon.

Bedding-plane: A horizontal break between two layers of sedimentation, bedding-planes are important in guiding the pattern of cave development.

Biospeleology: The scientific study of cave animal life.

Boulder choke: A pile of rocks and boulders that partly or wholly blocks a cave passage. This can be caused by debris being washed in from outside the cave, or from a collapse inside the cave (see Breakdown).

Boxwork: A checkerboard pattern resulting when cracked limestone fills with water-borne calcite.

Breakdown: A large accumulation of rock that blocks part or all of a passage after the collapse of part of the walls or ceiling.

Broomstick: Tall, thin stalagmites that resemble broom handles.

Calcite: Composed of calcium carbonate (calcium, carbon, and oxygen), calcite is the most common mineral found in caves and cave deposits. Limestone, chalk, and marble are composed of calcite. Pure calcite is white or colorless; minerals and impurities produce shades of pink, yellow, or brown. Calcite has the same composition as aragonite, but the atoms are arranged differently so the crystal structure and other properties also differ.

Calcium carbonate: This mineral, $CaCO_3$ (composed of calcium, carbon, and oxygen), occurs in nature as calcite and aragonite. It is the main ingredient in limestone, and is also found in plant ashes, bones, and shells.

Carbide lamp: A small headlamp used by miners and cavers. It is fueled when calcium carbide and water react to form acetylene gas, which then burns.

Catacomb cave: See Maze cave.

Cave: A naturally formed cavity or series of cavities in the ground, large enough to permit human entrance. Generally synonymous with "cavern."

Cave cauliflower: See Cave popcorn.

Cave coral: See Cave popcorn.

Cave deposit: An accumulation of material other than cave formations. This includes clay, gravel, charcoal, and fossils.

Cave grapes: See Cave popcorn.

Cave orchid: See Anthodite.

Cave pearls: Spherical or slightly irregular in shape, these objects form in pools where there is enough agitation (from dripping water) to prevent them from sticking to the bottom. Layers of calcite form around a nucleus of sand or a rock fragment, similar to the way a pearl develops in an oyster.

Cave popcorn: Small, irregular clusters of rounded formations composed of calcium carbonate. These stucco-like formations cover walls and surfaces (including other formations) that have been submerged in a pool or flooded chamber. Also known as cave cauliflower, cave grapes, and cave coral. Cave popcorn occurs most often along cracks or on porous silt deposits.

Cave system: Cavities and passages in a given area, which are now or once were connected.

Cavern: See Cave.

Column: A calcite cave formation that connects the floor and ceiling, this pillar-like structure occurs when a stalactite and a stalagmite join. (Columns can also be formed when a stalagmite grows all the way to the ceiling, or a stalactite gets long enough to meet the floor.) Water flowing down a column adds layers of flowstone to it, gradually enlarging it.

Conservation: The wise use of natural resources to preserve them for future generations.

Corrugated basins: See Rimstone dams.

Curtains: See Draperies.

Dogtooth spar: Large, pyramid-shaped crystals of pure calcium carbonate, formed under water in flooded or sealed chambers.

Domepit: A large, vertical underground shaft or corridor where water flowing down to the water table at a lower level has dissolved a cylindrical cavity in the rock, creating a dome above and a pit below.

Draperies: Thin and sometimes translucent hanging calcite formations shaped like a hanging sheet. A drapery formation begins when water flows down an inclined ceiling, leaving minerals behind. Some draperies have serrated edges like a knife blade, where each tooth is a crystal.

Dripstone: Cave deposits that have been formed by dripping water. Includes stalactites and stalagmites.

Echolocation: See Sonar.

Exoskeleton: An external skeleton, this is the hard body covering or shell of most invertebrates.

Fault: A fracture in the earth's crust accompanied by a displacement of one side of the fracture with respect to the other, parallel to the fracture.

Fissure: An open fracture in limestone formed along a bedding-plane, joint or fault. Usually a fissure is a narrow opening or long crack occurring from some breaking or parting.

Flowstone: Cave deposits formed as a result of water flowing over the surface. Often called travertine.

Formation: A term commonly used for secondary rock growth formed in a cave. This applies to dripstone and flowstone, but not to clay, gravel, charcoal, or fossils that are deposited.

Fossil: Any remains or traces of ancient animals or plants found in rock. These can be bones, tracks, imprints, or a mineral cast.

Geology: The scientific study of the history of the earth and the rocks that form it.

Gour barrier: The walls that gradually build up during the formation of rimstone dams.

Grotto: A cave chamber, usually small, decorated with calcite formations.

Guano: Sediment formed of animal droppings, mostly from bats.

Gypsum: A mineral composed of hydrated calcium sulphate that may form caves due to the solutional action of running water. Gypsum also appears as petal-like flower formations in drier limestone caves. These gypsum flowers grow from their bases, not their tips.

Helictite: A small, twisted calcite formation, deposited by water. Helictites can grow in any direction, including upward. Also called "eccentric stalactites," there are many theories about their origin. A probable explanation is that the capillary action of the water in a helictite's hollow center allows calcite crystals to form in irregular positions at the tip, giving the helictite its characteristic spiral shape.

Ice cave: A cave that contains ice formations throughout the year.

Karst: The typical topography and terrain of a limestone region, characterized by sinkholes, caves, and springs due to underground drainage. There is a general lack of surface water and much erosion, leaving no soil cover (or only a thin cover) over the limestone.

Knotty nodular forms: See Cave popcorn.

Lava cave or Lava tube: A tunnel formed where basaltic lava has recently flowed from a volcano. A tube is left when the outer layers solidify while the hot central zone drains away.

Limestone: A sedimentary rock, composed primarily of calcite. Limestone that contains caves was formed millions of years ago by the remains of marine plants and animals from ancient seas. These remains were compressed under pressure and cemented into rock, then uplifted and exposed to air and underground water. Because limestone is easily dissolved by carbon dioxide in water, caves are more common in limestone than in any other type of rock.

Maze cave: a complex system of cave passages most commonly formed along closely spaced joints in limestone.

Network cave: A complex cave system with many intersecting passages.

Organic: Pertaining to anything that is or ever was alive or produced by a living plant or animal. All organic matter contains the element carbon.

Paleontologist: A scientist who studies past life by analyzing and interpreting fossil remains of plants or animals.

Percolation water: Water that seeps slowly down through fractures in limestone.

Polymorphic: Occurring in various forms. For example, aragonite and calcite are polymorphs of calcium carbonate: they have the same content, but different atomic structures.

Pothole: A vertical-sided cave shaft, or a cave system with many of these shafts.

Rimstone dams and Rimstone pools: When water falls from stalactites, some of it may collect in pools or basins on the cave floor. As the water becomes saturated with calcium carbonate and overflows, it is slightly agitated, which causes carbon dioxide to be emitted. This results in calcium carbonate deposition at the edge of the basin, gradually building up wave-like, corrugated rims. Rimstone dams are often terraced like rice paddies, and enclose sizable pools of water.

Saltpeter: Mainly composed of nitrocalcite, saltpeter is one of the ingredients used to make gunpowder. This was mined in many southern Appalachian caves. Saltpeter silt was leached with water, then boiled with wood ashes to make niter.

Sandstone cave: Normally a shallow cave or rock shelter carved into the base of a cliff by water or wind erosion.

Sea cave: A cave formed by wave action on a shoreline where one part of the rock is more easily eroded than the adjacent rock.

Shale: A sedimentary rock formed of solidified mud, which commonly occurs as thin bands in limestone.

Shields: Semicircular, disk-shaped formations that project from walls or ceilings, often festooned with stalactites and draperies. They vary in size and in the position in which they occur. Shields appear riveted to the ceilings and side walls in a horizontal position. Each shield is made of two parallel plates separated by a fracture.

Sinkhole: A surface depression where a flow of water disappears into an underground cave. A sinkhole forms when the roof of a cave collapses or when limestone rock underlying the soil is slowly dissolved by water.

Soda straw: A stalactite with thin walls and a hollow center, having the approximate diameter of a drinking straw (about a quarter of an inch). Soda straws grow as water runs through their centers and deposits rings of calcite around their tips. All stalactites begin as soda straws.

Sonar: A system for detecting obstacles by emitting sound, then interpreting echoes that bounce back. It is used by bats and by some birds to navigate in caves.

Speleologist: A person who studies any of the scientific aspects of caves.

Speleothem: See Formation.

Spelunker: One who, as a hobby or for recreation, explores or studies caves.

Stalactite: A calcite formation hanging from the roof of a cave where it is deposited, dripping water that flows over the outside of a soda straw when the straw becomes plugged. Stalactites hang "tight" to the ceiling. (There's also a "c" for "ceiling" in the word.)

Stalagmite: A calcite formation that builds up from the floor of a cave, deposited by water dripping from above. Unlike the pointed tips of icicle-shaped stalactites, the tops of stalagmites are blunt and rounded. Stalagmites "might" make it up to the ceiling some day. (There's also a "g" for "ground" in the word.)

Streamway: A passage with a stream flowing along it.

Travertine: Calcium carbonate deposited from solution in underground and surface waters. This term encompasses cave deposits such as stalactites, stalagmites, dripstone, and flowstone.

Troglobite: A permanently cave-dwelling animal.

Twilight zone: The area of a cave where light from the entrance is enough for human vision.

Water table: The drainage level in rock below which all fissures are completely saturated with water, and above which fissures are only partly filled.